WHERE GRANDPA'S BEEN...

An Autobiography

Dr. Donald Huard

authorHOUSE®

AuthorHouse™
1663 Liberty Drive
Bloomington, IN 47403
www.authorhouse.com
Phone: 1 (800) 839-8640

Published by AuthorHouse 04/09/2015

ISBN: 978-1-5049-0264-9 (sc)
ISBN: 978-1-5049-0263-2 (e)

Library of Congress Control Number: 2015904547

Print information available on the last page.

This book is printed on acid-free paper.

To my grandchildren:

Bobby Dean, Nathan, Cortney
Aaron, Tyler, Lindsay, Lauren, Brandon
Jeremy, Stacia, Heather, Ryan
Rebecca, Julie, Hannah, Sarah, Jonathan
Derek, Ann

And my great grandchildren:

Sierra, Austin
Nathane, Michael
Gianna, Dylan
Alora, Ryland
Rowen, Alexandria

The Author wishes to express his appreciation to his daughter,

Theresa Ann Huard Bullock,

a skilled medical and legal transcriptionist who contributed so much of her time and her love while formatting the manuscript of my book for publication.

Contents

Introduction

When I was a young man in my early thirties, sharing the burden of raising four pre-teen children with my wife Marie, I so often thought about how old I would be one distant day when mankind entered the new millennium. I had it figured out that I would be sixty-seven years old when the twenty-first century began. Then, the millennium was many years away. As the year 2000 arrived I would be a retired citizen with nearly forty years of experience as a husband, parent and educational psychologist. That was way off in the distant future, when I would be old and grey.

What I didn't know when our children were young was that the next thirty years would go by as though they took only a single decade. It's astounding to discover that you have become an older person well before you had planned it. Teaching in the classroom month after month, year after year while watching our pre-teens become teenagers, then young adults, then full grown mature adults with their own little children made us focus on them rather than ourselves. Oblivious to time, I became an old grey-haired grandpa before I realized what was happening.

How was I to know when I was thirty that my first marriage would end just after I turned fifty? How was I to know that the loss of Marie to illness in 1981, would be followed by what I have since referred to as a "super second" life?

How could I have imagined during the pain of the loss of my children's mom that a new life was to follow, one that is also filled with love and devotion, a marriage of great good fortune for me that, in its thirtieth year continues to grow in strength and in commitment?

It is my intention to write my insignificant little story as a positive reflection of the wonderful things that have happened to me throughout my lifetime with a little less emphasis on the sad parts and a greater emphasis on the good things that have made my life worthwhile and ultimately quite fulfilling.

The wonderful feeling of a life well lived, children well raised, career objective attained and contributions made to others serves as sufficient reward for prices paid. Many times, throughout my later years, I have thought about the responsibility I have to convey a positive mental outlook about life to my children. Life is too short to be lived unhappily or experienced as a cross to bear, shrouded in martyred servitude. Life is to be lived joyously, the early years lived with a willing enthusiasm for challenge. The mature years should be rich with contentment and the power of positive reflection.

On the pages that follow, you will find my expressions of gratitude to the people who influenced me in a positive way, to those who raised me, those who pushed me along, those who helped me pick myself up when clobbered by life and those who assured me that they appreciated my efforts.

For what they are worth, I'll include a few reflections about life that have taken over eighty years to develop, years that went by so quickly that the millennium arrived over fifteen years ago. One thing is sure, the attitudes I held when I was just a boy of twenty changed significantly through my thirties, forties and fifties, so much so that I am clearly not the same person today. The old man is more than just the youth plus the passage of time.

The major motivation for this book, however, is to be found in my determination to effectively communicate much about my life to my children and grandchildren. Maybe my own children will come to recognize and accept the fact that when I was a young parent to them and a bit less attendant to their special needs and interests, I was fighting some of my own demons and dragons.

I hope as they read this book, they will find reason to be proud of me, as I am of them. I hope they will be proud of grandpa for his fighting spirit. I hope they will understand and be forgiving toward him in spite of his preoccupations. Above all, I hope they will be loving toward him during his declining years.

Chapter One

The Huards

For children born in the 30s (1932 for me) the early school years were marked by a national preoccupation with winning the wars with Germany and Japan. Many children were raised with their daddies away. Many fathers didn't return. During the early years of the 1940s many of the moms in America spent the duration working in factories building field guns and tanks or in large aircraft hangers hammering rivets into the bodies of fighter planes and bombers.

Everyday commodities such as sugar, coffee, meat and gasoline were hard to come by during the war. They were needed by the soldiers and sailors who were fighting to keep the world free. Ration stamps were needed to get those things for any family. Every home featured a box of crushed tin cans, toothpaste tubes and paper saved for recycling to support the war effort. Children filled their wagons with old newspapers and pulled them to their school yards. They collected used rubber tires and anything made of any kind of metal that could be melted down and made into new parts for trucks, ships and planes.

To mom and dad that was the big war. More wars were to follow, but that was the big one. Casualty statistics for World War II show how right they were when they made that claim. Compared to the Korean conflict during which 34,000 American military personnel were killed and the Vietnam War that took 58,000, the deaths got to over 407,000 between the years of 1941 and 1945! In Africa, Italy,

France and Germany allied troops beat the Germans into submission, at a tremendous cost in human life.

After the devastating attack on the American fleet at Pearl Harbor in Hawaii on December 7, 1941 and the island hopping invasion of the Philippines by the Japanese it took a year to turn the tide of the war in the South Pacific. Two decisive sea battles, one at the Coral Sea in May of 1942 and another at Midway just one month later resulted in such huge naval losses for the Japanese that they were unable to launch any assaults on Hawaii. As a child, I was unable to understand the reason for the wars. Why were we fighting? A boy of ten couldn't understand the why…

Still, in the South Pacific it took several years of very fierce fighting to push the Japanese back toward their own mainland. American, British, Canadian and Australian ground forces were mauled by invaders during the earliest part of the war. The enemy eventually lost their control over the Philippines and over virtually all of Southeast Asia as the allied forces led by General Douglas McArthur returned in great force. After the end of the war, the Philippine Sea was dominated by the U.S. Fleet under the sound direction of Vice Admiral Chester William Nimitz, commander of Central Pacific Operations.

Mom and dad called it the big war. Fierce battles for islands like Tarawa, Saipan, Corregador, Iwo Jima and Okinawa are legend for their significance in the winning of the war. However, the coup de grace came during the week of August 6 - 12th, 1945 when American B-29 bombers dropped two atomic bombs on Hiroshima and Nagasaki. Immediate deaths on just Horoshima alone on a single day equaled 66,000, more than the total number of deaths of American troops during the entire Vietnam War.

Of course, I was just a child when all this was happening. I was nine years old at the beginning and thirteen when it ended. Mom and dad were raising their six children in Dearborn, Michigan at the time. Dad worked as a design draftsman and electrical engineer for the General Motors Company before the war, but automobiles were not built during 1942 through 1945 because the industries turned to the production of war materials. During the war dad worked on field artillery guns, frequently traveling to Aberdine, Maryland for consultations with military personnel.

George and Viola Huard (mom was the former Viola Margaret Lucier) were truly dedicated parents. Catholic to the core, they had most of their kids registered into Saint Alphonsus School on Warren Avenue at Shaffer Road in Dearborn. We went to church every Sunday, made our first communions right on schedule and went to confession for our sins at least once a month.

Ray (George R. Huard, Jr.) was the oldest of the six children. He was a very capable student who excelled at drawing and drafting and the building of magnificently detailed model airplanes and, of all things for a young fellow, a lover of classical music. Ray has always been a fine role model for the rest of us. He lives presently, at age eighty-six, in Palo Alto, California where he spent his working years as a single man and a draftsman for some space and computer oriented businesses in Silicon Valley.

Shirley is just one year younger than Ray. A delightfully pretty high school girl with auburn hair and an outgoing personality, she naturally drew lots of special friends to our large Dearborn home. Shirley left our family at about the age of twenty-four, moving to Southern California, where she married an Irish fellow by the name of Joseph Patrick Sweeney, who became the father of their three children, Michael, Kelly and Patrick. Mike became a skilled musician who plays the bassoon for the Ontario Symphony in Canada. Kelly has recently completed the requirements for her master's degree in education and is a sixth grade teacher. Patrick is an x-ray technician.

Richard and his wife Margaret raised a family in Dearborn. As a young man, Rich, as we called him, was into cars, trucks and even for awhile, horses. He took some body and fender repair classes in high school and did some astounding auto redesign projects over the years. In his young twenties he was doing chop channel work on deuce coupes, Pontiac sedans, etc., as a hobby that stayed with him for sixty years. He served in the U.S. Army near the end of the big war, followed by a long career with the Ford Motor Company in Dearborn, where he worked as a skilled technician. Richard and Marge had three children,

Robert, Sandy and Terry. Bob is following his dad's work history at Ford Motor. Sandy works for the Terminex Company. Terry is a brake service specialist for a truck maintenance company.

Mary moved to San Diego, California with her husband Paul Brown in 1950. The couple divorced several years after the birth of their daughter Debby and mom and daughter came to Phoenix, Arizona. Years later she married Roy Schmidt, a swimming pool service man who passed away in 1984. Mary died in 2010.

Ken is the youngest of the George and Viola Huard family. He's seventy years old now, a retired machinist. He received his early machinist training while on tour in Germany with the U.S. Army. He lives in Gilbert, Arizona. Ken and his former wife raised two children, Lisa and Ken, Jr.

Where do *I* fit into this family of six catholic kids parented by George and Viola? Well, I like to think of myself as a middle kid. But how can there be a middle kid in a family of six? I seem to be the one who got lost somewhere between the oldest and the youngest. It wasn't bad. I wasn't mistreated or anything. I think that I must have had a good upbringing, as I turned out so well (?). I can't blame anyone else for what I did and didn't become.

I remember the big war a little bit. Too young to serve in the war, I finished grade school in an unimpressive way, disliking the nuns. In eighth grade I fell in love with Rose Marie somebody, a girl who was more impressed by Sinatra than me. For a short while, I wondered why… I remember some things - the blue and white banners that hung in the windows of parents whose sons served in the war. The gold ones representing a soldier or sailor lost.

I delivered a still existing local afternoon newspaper called the Detroit Free Press when I was about eleven. It took me and my wheels through the neighborhoods, tossing folded editions under porches and onto roof tops, collecting $.35 for a week's delivery. I remember riding in the dark one morning yelling "EXTRA-EXTRA - Roosevelt dies!" Porch lights came on and I got my nickel at the door, handed out a paper and I could see the crying adults crowding around their old floor model RCA radios in the living rooms. Americans were stunned by the thought that their beloved four-time elected president Franklin Delano Roosevelt (FDR) had died without being able to see the end of the big war.

I was a kid who loved mechanical things, cameras and motors of all sorts, especially. Ray helped me to enclose a little space under the stairway to the basement where we developed black and white pictures. Three little 5" X 7" blue and white trays held the developer, short stop and hypo used to reveal the dynamic images that I recorded with my Kodak box camera that I later took with me when I was drafted into the U.S. Army. Ray eventually set up a real neat darkroom in the basement coal bin, complete with a home-made enlarger he constructed out of a potato chip can and a bellows camera so that we could astound the rest of the family and our friends with our wizardry! I loved Ray and Richard, and still do. As big brothers, they were the greatest!

When I was fourteen, Richard let me drive his old model A Ford sedan for a block or two. I was fascinated by the bubble gas gauge and the seats that folded in half, then upward near the dash board to let someone ride in the back seat. I couldn't believe that *that* car could go 55 miles per hour! Richard took me to Hillsdale, Michigan a few times in his stake truck to buy horses for a local feed company. I loved watching Rich bid for horses, loved watching him coax them on board for the ride back home to Dearborn.

Those were the days when I worked as a caddy for the golfers at the Dearborn Country Club, learning that even the wealthy paid only the rate of $1.15 to any eager kid who would carry a heavy bag full of fancy clubs for eighteen holes of duffer frustration. I was delighted to find that the richest golfers seemed to be the very worst golfers. My delight in finding this out may have come from my experiences of having several of them vent their anger at their caddy.

The trauma and pressures of the war, the heavy responsibilities of being the father of six children and the husband of an overly disciplined catholic wife much inclined toward deep depression began to take a toll on one George Huard, Sr. in his own middle forties. So did the terrible cold, wet winters in Michigan, terrible not for the young and healthy but much more so for those with dad's special medical problems. He experienced the increasing immobilizing effects of muscular rheumatism and arthritis.

Progressive in nature, these afflictions resulted in his use of a cane when he walked. Eventually, the problem became so severe that he was forced to quit his good job of twenty-one years at the Cadillac Division of General Motors. I can remember the very day that dad's bed was moved downstairs into the living room because our saintly mom found it easier to care for him on a low level not involving his painful climbing up the stairs to get to the bedroom. I remember watching him go up and down those stairs in a sitting position, moving slowly trying to ease his pain.

Remembering dad's age at any given time was never a problem for us. He was born in 1900, so in 1920 he was twenty years of age. In 1940, he was forty. In his mid-forties, he was devastated by arthritis, forced to give up his major career association and his income, forced to find a new life-style at a time when his responsibilities were the greatest in his life.

A little better for awhile, dad tried an entirely new employment direction. Feeling that he might do a little better doing outside work, he purchased a nice new dark blue Dodge panel truck, had the logo "Westown Cleaners" printed on its side and served his family by picking up and delivering dry cleaning in the Dearborn neighborhoods. I recall helping him on his delivery route and I imagine that my big brothers must have done so as well. Cold winters and the high summer humidity continued to adversely affect his muscles and inflamed joints, however. It wasn't very long before it became obvious that the new job would not help.

Imagine our surprise when, one evening at the long supper table with the full family of eight present for a big family talk, our dad and mom told us that the doctors were recommending that the family leave dear old Dearborn and move to some place with a climate more conducive to potential recovery of those who suffered from osteoarthritis. "ARIZONA," we all wailed? "That's where the Indians are. What about leaving our friends? Where will we go to school," we asked? "What about my friends, Loma Lee, and Arlene," Shirley asked? "What about my friend Jake and my girlfriend Pauline," Richard asked? "Sure as Hell won't miss the nuns at Saint Al's," Ray quipped.

It must have been a difficult decision that mom and dad made, involving the uprooting of their kids from school and their friends, selling the Dearborn home, the transporting of a family of eight to a land strange and far away in hopes of a recovery for dad that might or might not occur. Ray, the oldest, was about twenty-two at the time. Ken, the baby, was only three. Because we loved our father and we knew something had to change, we reluctantly joined forces for the move. November of 1947, the entire Huard family set out for a new life for us all, amidst the desert scorpions and the red rocks of Central Arizona. It proved to be quite a trip...

At the top: Dad, Donald and Ray

with

Shirley, Kenny, Mary, Mom and Richard

The Huard Family
in 1947

Chapter Two

Westward Ho !

Imagine the courage it must have taken to sell a home lived in for twenty years and pack up a family of eight and move them all two thousand miles away to a new life, especially considering the fact that the patriarch of the family was so ill that he had to ride most of the way lying flat on a mattress in the back of his panel truck. That was the challenge faced by George and Viola Huard and their kids, Ray, Shirley, Richard, Donald (me), Mary and Ken in November of 1947.

It took lots of planning and lots of determination. Dad could drive some, but most of the driving responsibility fell to the kids. Mom never did drive, so Ray, Shirley and Richard drove the three vehicles in our "caravan" through nine states over eleven days before we reached the relatively small city of Phoenix, Arizona. I had just turned fifteen in May of that year so I was not old enough to drive. Of course, I wanted to, but dad wouldn't hear of it. He was right. Way back then, there were laws that people respected. Besides, we didn't need any trouble with the law to add to our other miseries. It took awhile to sell a six room house on Ternes Avenue in Dearborn, but it had to be done to free up funds for the move. Dad got the idea that if he bought a house trailer to pull along behind the new blue Dodge panel truck we would not only have a place to live in on the road and after we got to our new destination in the Valley of the Sun. Then we could sell it.

House trailers then were not like the mobile homes of today. Nor were they like the motor homes that you see on the today's highways.

They were more likely to be those small, square single axle units only eight feet wide, and in the case of the one owned by the Huards, just twenty-seven feet long including the tow bar. Who would think today of moving a family the size of ours all the way across the country without any job prospects or any idea about where to settle down or what church to go to? How to fit a group of eight into a trailer with a mini-closet for a bathroom? Well, you do what you gotta do… Often in the bushes along the highway.

Let's see, mom and dad will get the 6 foot 8 inch x 7 foot 6 inch "master" bedroom, Shirl and Mary will sleep in the tiny bedroom, Ray and Rich will sleep in the hallway by the heating unit. Don will sleep in the kitchen, his head next to the refrigerator compressor that goes on, off and on and off and Ken will sleep in the kitchen sink. What else could anyone ask for?

Ray drives the Dodge truck that pulls the trailer. Richard will follow the panel truck and trailer in his forty Ford stake truck used for hauling horses, now filled with six rooms of furniture from the Dearborn house. Meanwhile, Shirl, with dad serving as relief driver to the extent that his aching body will permit, will drive the family's forty Chevy loaded with food and clothes needed by the eight of us, plus one mom, Mary and baby Kenny. I will ride sometimes with Ray, sometimes with Rich, and, for variety, occasionally with Shirley, when Mary rides with Ray or Rich. It's all so easy, you know, if you just plan it. Mom will cook us great meals along the road and we will stop at gas stations to use the potties. Never had it so good!

At night we'll find a trailer park where we can hook up the electricity (we really should buy a generator) and use the community bathrooms and showers. People do this sort of thing all of the time. It should be a blast, goin' west just like the explorers who traveled in covered wagons. I'll take along a new B-B gun just in case we need to fight off mountain lions or Indians.

That first day lots of cheering neighbors watched as the Huards eased away from the grey shingled, two story home of our youth, never more to see the basement filled with cornstalks for Halloween parties. Never more to gasp for air in a basement filled with smoke from the running of tiny model airplane engines that used to drive mom to distraction.

No more rusty tin cans used to catch pollywogs at the local creek or riding cardboard down the icy hill near the overpass on Warren Avenue by the Brazis Grocery Store. Never again would we go tobogganing or ski down the slope at River Rouge Park or ice skate over at the frozen creek pond. Never again would I play baseball with my old friends or get clobbered by another line drive hit by a buddy that darkened my two front teeth.

We would never again use the local passenger train only a block away, the one we called the "*streamliner*" to flatten pennies on the track. We would never again hear the synchronized chant of the men called the "*gandy dancers*" who grunted in unison as they used their pry bars to align the tracks.

There was cranky old Mrs. Iva Mersdorf, actually smiling as we left. I didn't like that lady. She would threaten to call the police if we walked on her lawn. The Miskies across the street waved as our caravan edged its way out of town. Mrs. Miskie must have been still mad at me for burning off the eyebrows and lashes of her son Danny. Richard had an old parts car that sat on the lot next door. One day I dropped a match in the gasoline intake tube, not knowing Danny would look down into it to see if it was still lit. It was! The explosion blew the bottom out of the tank. Up top, it damned near blew Danny's head off!

His mamma Miskie had no sense of humor when it came to her Danny. She charged over and screamed at mom for what I did. It was okay though, six months later her Daniel was as good as new. A half hour later as we left the Barrie Drug Store five blocks away some folks asked us what that loud noise was that they heard. I guess some of the neighbors were glad to see the Huards go.

As we left town, we took one last look at the Allen Fence Company that I tried to burn down on the fourth of July when I was about ten. I threw a firecracker onto a pile of wood in their yard that ignited some boards. I hid under mom and dad's bed when I heard the fire trucks coming to put out the fire. I feared the police were coming to take me to jail. Dumb kid!

Then we bid a happy adieu to Saint Al's very catholic school. No more Sister Innertube (Inatrude?), the Darth Vader look-alike nun who beat my forehead with that algebra book. Thank God, no more Latin! Will mom finally stop taking us to confession? We didn't make it very far that first day. We were too exhausted just from beginning our trip. Our first stop was on the outskirts of the city of Toledo, Ohio where we found a place to set up so that we would have water and electricity for the night. Mom got the hang of the propane stove quite quickly so that we could have hot soup and other quick meals before turning in.

Getting the eight of us settled down for a night was itself a big chore. There was always one more who needed to go to the bathroom and couldn't find the flashlight. It was always very cold in the night and coats and sweaters were often left in the car. The kids wanted to giggle, the grown-ups wanted to sleep. The trailer was too hot for the men, too cold for the women. Kenny was only three and would get cranky. Mom tended to step on the kids lying on the floor in the hallway and kitchen. You couldn't open the refrigerator door when Don's head was in the way.

Dad wanted us up very early the next morning. We all wanted to sleep. Breakfast time was an impossible challenge for mom and Shirley who tried to help with eggs or pancakes. That damned trailer door slammed over and over as kids ran in and out. Dishes should be washed and also stashed so they wouldn't break when we were on the road. There wasn't enough silverware. Soon we ate on paper plates, using plastic spoons, forks and kiddie fingers.

Next, an all-day drive southward toward Indianapolis, Indiana. Truck and trailer first, followed by the stake truck, then Shirley in the Chevy. The weather was quite good considering that it was the month of November. But oh, so cold at night! I don't know how he did it with his body hurting so, but dad kept our spirits up, assuring us that it would be nice and warm in Arizona. Little did we know how warm it could get in the desert country.

The trip was not without mishaps. The first night the trailer was backed into a tree in the trailer court, causing a broken bumper. No biggie, 2 x 4s make good bumpers that are very easy to replace. No fancy chrome on this trailer. What could have been a tragedy nearly happened on the road the next day. On a rather narrow two-lane highway a semi-truck approached our caravan as we descended down into a canyon. Unaware of a problem, the driver came at us at sixty miles per hour with the rear door of his trailer flying open and whipping over into the lane we were using. The hinges were broken and the door swung at us as though on a chain.

God was with us on that day. That door swung over our lane as we all went into a panic! Then it swung behind the semi to let Ray and dad go by, just missing our truck and trailer. It swung again over the lane then back out of sight, letting Richard's truck pass through. It missed Shirley, Mary, mom and Ken in the car as well. If that door had hit any of our vehicles, surely some of us would have died that day. Mom never knew how close we had been to eternity. If she had known, we surely would have been going to confession in Saint Louis.

After a night outside of Saint Louis and another near Memphis, Tennessee, we were all beginning to get a bit edgy. Mom and dad fought a bit, the kids kept teasing and poking one another and there were always two who needed a potty stop. We were getting mighty tired of lunchmeat, tired of being so confined and tired of each other.

Amidst flares of temper there was lots of laughter. One night as we got settled and were just about to fall asleep dad reached up to close a blind over the bed wanting to block out the light of the Tennessee moon, when the blind fell to the floor making a loud crashing sound. Dad swore at it and we all chuckled. Just then, as though on signal, a donkey in a nearby field brayed "Hee-haw!" It took an extra half hour to get us all settled down that night.

My BB gun nearly got me killed one afternoon in a place right on the Arkansas-Texas border called Texarkana. We stopped our driving a little early that day and rested in a little trailer park on the edge of town. The sun was still up after we got hooked up and a bored kid took a Daisy gun out back of the park over on the far side of a large hill to shoot at targets, twigs and cans.

Suddenly, a large man came running past me in a panic, nearly knocking me down as he threw himself in a ravine at the base of the hill. As I watched him stagger into the bushes and trees, I was startled by a very loud "BANG" that nearly knocked me down again. On the top of the hill, running toward me was a police officer, gun in hand, firing at the bad guy. Then he fired again as he chased the man down the ravine.

We learned later that the fellow had robbed a service station near the trailer park and was eventually cornered up near the highway where he was shot to death by another officer. By that time I had run back to our trailer. Terrified, I told mom and dad what had happened.

Dad's reaction to my tale was characterized by a panic that I had never seen before in my gentle, loving father. He grabbed me, hauled me behind the trailer and began scolding me for shooting that damned gun. Then he took the gun away from me. Dad yelled at me while poking his finger into my chest so deep that I thought I was being stabbed. "Do you know that cop could have killed you," he screamed? "There he was, shooting at that guy, and you were standing there with a rifle in your hands."

It was the only time in my entire life that dad had been that mean to me. I was upset for weeks over that. Even the next day, when he apologized to me, I was unable to forgive him. I didn't feel that I had done anything wrong. It took a long time for me to understand that dad had simply lost control of his own fear that afternoon when his son was in such danger. It took becoming a father myself to make me realize that love for your own child goes so deep and becomes so overwhelming that you aren't always in control.

It took a long time to learn just how much dad loved me and all of his other kids, how dedicated he and mom were to keeping us all safe and secure. It took me lots of years facing my own parenting responsibilities to understand why he, already tortured by arthritic pain and fatigue in the middle of that exhausting trip, had come apart one afternoon. It took evolution into adulthood to see what a great father I had. Even now, sixty years later the memory of that day makes me cry.

Abilene, Texas next, happily without any major incident. We had taken the southern route across the country and were only a few days from our destination. No blown tires, no severely sick kids, no engine failures, no major snowstorms. Just the cold at night, the endless miles of boredom, the constant hunt for rest stops and more and more "maloney" sandwiches.

We spent one day across the border from El Paso in dry, old Juarez, Mexico. It was hot, crowded and dirty and we were glad to get back to our "luxurious" home. We got lost in New Mexico. Dad's favorite traveling phrase was "You can't get there from here, you have to go there first. Then you can get there from there - if you can find it." We got separated from Richard's stake truck for hours and we didn't know which of us was on the wrong road. Finally, we decided to turn the Chevy around and backtrack. We found Richard laughing his head off with a skunk eatn' dirt grin on his face as he leaned against a huge highway sign that read "Welcome to Arizona."

Eleven days. That's how long it took George and Viola's caravan to get to Phoenix, Arizona. We hooked up at the Michigan Trailer Park on Grand Avenue. "Next we'll get a nice house, sell the trailer, get started in our new schools and find some new friends." We'll even find a church for confession. Maybe, just maybe, dad will start to feel better...

Chapter Three

Settling In and Falling Down

The little trailer seemed to shrink in size as the weeks went by. We stayed at the Michigan Trailer Park on the west side of Phoenix for only a week or so. The park seemed to be more for overnighters and truckers who were just passing through, not for long-term family living as in a true mobile home setting. Dad recognized this rather quickly and he began to investigate the parts of the city that seemed to have stable neighborhoods, places where we might consider the purchase of a home.

We moved the trailer to a very small park in a very small place called the Devonshire Trailer Park located on the east side near Indian School Road and 12th Street. It was cheaper to rent a space on a monthly basis than to continue paying for overnight hookups as we did that first week. Fortunately, the Longview Elementary School was only three blocks away and North Phoenix high School was at Thomas Road, one mile away.

Ray, Shirley and Richard were out of high school then. I was just beginning my freshman year and Mary was in the sixth grade. Kenny was just a toddler at the time. It didn't take long before Mary and I were enrolled in the public schools where we were taught by teachers who looked like everybody else.

Still, that trailer was getting smaller and smaller. We were getting more and more in each other's way and mom was clawing at the walls for more space. Think of it this way - the trailer was 27 feet long, but the hitch took up three feet so there was actually only 24 feet times eight feet of floor space. A single bedroom apartment often occupied by one or two people today is expected to have over 500 square feet of floor space and seem a bit small. We had eight people living in a trailer with only 192 square feet of living area!

Is it any wonder that mom and dad were so desperate to find a home in a hurry? They didn't have to look for long. One day dad took mom to look at a *huge* two-bedroom, 900 square foot home with a living room, a dining room, a *huge* kitchen (as compared to the one in the trailer) and one *huge* four foot by six foot bathroom (with a bathtub). It was on Meadowbrook Avenue near the northern edge of town. Mom walked in the front door, took a quick look and said, "This is it! And that was that.

Mom and dad got the master bedroom. Shirley and Mary got the other bedroom. Ray, Richard, Donald and Kenny got the living and dining area and mom got to cook in a kitchen without stepping on me. See how good things come to those who wait?

After moving all of the furniture from the huge house in Dearborn into the *huge* house in Phoenix by selling much of it, Richard's stake truck was empty again at last. He hauled groceries for awhile for the Smart & Final food chain, but missed his friends back home in Dearborn so he went back there to live. It wasn't long before he met and married Margie and they raised three children.

Ray got a draftsman's job at Motorola. He didn't stay long in Phoenix. He couldn't stand the summers in 115 degree heat. Off to Palo Alto, California, a good career in draftsmanship as a job shopper, a love for fly fishing for trout in the local streams and an ever-persistent passion for his endless love - golf.

I remember when Shirley left the Phoenix roost to make a new life for herself in Los Angeles. She was just about twenty-four at the time. I remember it well because Jimmie Klink and I took her there in my old 1938 Ford with the slipping clutch. It was the only car I ever had that would race its engine for no reason whatever, even when it was in gear and you didn't have your foot on the clutch. Getting the clutch to hold its grip when we climbed hills was a challenge.

We hunted around town until we found a nice boarding house that seemed reasonably respectable where she could live and make some new friends. It was an unimpressive place filled with other young folks setting out for their independence. Shirley was in conflict over whether or not she belonged there and at one point asked if she shouldn't change her mind and go back to Phoenix with us. We assured her that if she stayed there for awhile but did change her mind we would "slip" back over to get her.

To Shirley's considerable credit, she did stay, got a job with a place called Monsanto Chemical and was soon living in a nice apartment of her own. Back in Phoenix, we missed Shirley a lot. My big sister had helped me cope with a lot of teenage trauma and I missed the long discussions of why I was no longer loved and why I had to go to high school when all I wanted was to work, get a better car and get rich…

The home in Phoenix had grown in just a year or so. Dad, Ray, Rich and I had added a third bedroom in back of the house that eased the crowding a bit until the family split with one going back home and two living in California. The family that remained included dad, mom, me, Mary and Kenny.

A most amazing thing happened! Dad's joint aches and muscle pains began to ease in the dry Arizona Heat. He would lie out in the backyard being cooked day after day. He began to enjoy life again. I remember a day when I saw something I could hardly believe. Dad was actually up on the roof of the house and was working on the cooler!

Dad was getting well. His evenings were spent reading his paper and smoking his pipe as he relaxed in comfort in his easy chair (round-topped RCA console radio nearby) instead of in twisting agony as he had done in Dearborn. Today I would love to be the proud owner of that little walnut pipe rack and tobacco stand that he loved so much. I used to watch him cut up pieces of apple to put in his tobacco pouch to keep his Prince Albert moist.

It wasn't long before dad began to realize that the money supply was dwindling, that he had to get income coming in again. There were no automobile plants in the new city. He was getting better, but still was not strong. The boys were still at home when dad decided to buy out the remaining stock from a defunct hardware store and set up his own business. He met a young man who was operating an air-conditioning service out of one side of a building located on 7th Street at Camelback Road, the northernmost, east-west paved road in town. Charles Robert's Air Conditioning was to become one of the major businesses in the scorched Phoenix area through the 50s and remains as a large and thriving enterprise today.

With the help of his sons, dad became the proud proprietor of George's Hardware, located in the other half of the building owned by Charlie Roberts. At $125 per month the rent was reasonable, the location was perfect, and the stock, including everything from tools to brackets, from wheelbarrows to nails to paints to garbage cans to pots and pans made for an attractive store run by a friendly, honest man who sincerely wanted to do right by his customers.

I was just sixteen then and my big brothers were leaving. My days consisted of school attendance in the mornings and work in the store after three-thirty each afternoon. I worked all day Saturdays. I would often close the store at six o'clock and pedal my bike home. In the winter time it would mean a long five-block trip alone down Highland Avenue in the dark.

I was a troubled young man at that time. I was bored by schoolwork, so I did everything possible to avoid any serious consideration of it. My grades were terrible and my attitude must have been worse. I did try hard for dad, though, and I knew he appreciated it. He was remarkably understanding and considerate of this young son who was always interested in "other things."

Dad would send me downtown to the supply warehouses for supplies in the Chevy and I learned a lot about order forms, delivery receipts and inventory control. Sometimes I would spend half a day at Arizona Sales, Black & Ryan and other sources of supply. We had sold the panel truck by then, so the old pre-war Chevy became the workhorse for our hardware business. I hauled paint, kegs of nails, shovels and rakes, boxed bicycles and everything else in that car.

On one of those warehouse trips I brought back two new Rollfast bikes that dad had me assemble in the front of the store. It was late in the day when I finished the second one and I noticed that for some reason mom had shown up at the store. With her watching, dad yanked the

$39.95 price tag off of the second bike and said, "This one's for you, son." I was thrilled with my new bike, but let me tell a secret. I sort of wished it had been equipped with a Whizzer motor, because I loved engines and loved working on them. Of course, I didn't say that to dad. I didn't want to appear ungrateful. It was a neat bike.

Dad did love his Chevy. We tried to keep it in good shape as it was also the "Go to confession" car for the family as well. Imagine his frustration when I returned to the store one Saturday afternoon having driven all the way from downtown with my head out the driver's side window, gasping for air because I had broken a full gallon bottle of muriatic acid and spilled it all over the rear seat and floor. All chemicals were in glass jugs (or cans) then. There were no plastic containers. We actually had to hose out the inside of his car! It's amazing that he didn't take my head off. He didn't.

Then there were many times when I would ride my bike home in the dark, guarding the little box that carried the last of the day's receipts, having forgotten to bring in the shovel rack, bikes and wheelbarrows that we used as inducements to drivers who traveled 7th Street during business hours. Sometimes as late as 10 o'clock at night our doorbell would ring and a policeman would be standing on the porch asking dad if he knew that Don had forgotten his responsibility to batten down the hatches again!

Dad would get in the car, drive back to the store and bring things inside as God intended. He was constantly trying to get "other occupied" son (me) to tend to business.

Typically for any teenager, the things that really occupied my consciousness were motors, cars and girls. There just wasn't anything else in the world that was worthy of my attention, certainly not schoolwork, certainly not my chores, clearly not babysitting Mary and Kenny and definitely not going to church for, well, you know…

Then it happened. Or, should I say *she* happened. Sharon. Oh, Sharon! She was the most gorgeous fifteen-year-old sweetheart that any sixteen-year-old fellow could ever have hoped to find after all of his years of searching. She was beautifully tall, stunningly pretty, wonderfully graceful, incredibly mature, genuinely sincere and naturally sweet.

Just another ordinary teenage kid, isn't that right? Well, not to the uninitiated, hopelessly vulnerable, acne-punctured kid who walked her home from school each day.

Falling in love the first time is like tumbling down the basement stairs on your tricycle. It's quite a ride. It's exciting. It's painful. It's daring. It's dangerous. It's startling, frightening and can be devastating. It's wonderful and awful at the same time. All in all, it's unbelievably stupid. If I had known then what I know now, I would have been too embarrassed to be involved. I most surely wouldn't have wanted anybody to see me acting so silly.

You can't think straight when you are in love for the first time. It's tough enough the second or third time. But those later times you can at least build in some protections for yourself in case your romance hits the skids. Not that first time. No. That one is gonna last forever.

So it was gonna be with Sharon and idiot Donnie in the early 50s. It's no wonder that I kept showing up late for my afternoon job at the hardware store. Is it any wonder that I kept forgetting the garbage cans and the wheelbarrows out in front of the store at closing time? Is it any wonder that I couldn't concentrate on algebra? All I could think of was Sharon.

Sharon's mom and dad ran the neighborhood grocery store on 12th Street only a block from our house. It was a nice, well-run neighborhood grocery that came with a soda fountain where Sharon made the best acne-enhancing chocolate sodas in the west.

They didn't like me much, for two reasons. One was that I was (gasp) catholic - they were protestant. The other was that I was a skinny motorbike crazed punk who cleaned the oil out of his hair only for Christmas and Easter.

Sharon's dad was an interesting man. He was the type who liked to shoot his deer rifle into the air at midnight on New Year's Eve. One afternoon just after I left his daughter, she called me in a panic. She had found that loaded rifle in the living room next to her dad's chair, picked it up and proceeded to blow a hole in the dining room wall. I often thought he might come after me with that gun.

Her mother thought that Sharon and I were getting too serious so she coerced daddy to come down to the house to talk to my mom. In front of her, he told me to stay away from Sharon. Sweet, little, saintly mom of mine told him to go to hell! I told him if Sharon wanted me to I would. She didn't.

Sharon and I went to the football games together, a few proms together and graduated from high school together in 1951. She was an honor student. I, on the other hand, graduated 395th in the class of 410. We even dated without her folks knowing it by having a friend of mine pick her up and take her home. Now, I'm not proud of our youthful subterfuge.

At the urging of her parents, I suppose intent on getting her away from me, that awful, worthless boyfriend of hers, Sharon went off to San Francisco for six weeks of molar training at a dental nursing school. Her parents would have been apoplectic had they known that I followed her up there for a few days in the middle of her semester. When I got back I wanted to go over to the soda fountain and tell her mother that Sharon was doing fine. I didn't. She graduated with honors and came home looking even more beautiful in her new white uniform and cap. I was still overwhelmed by her.

Dad's hardware store failed. It was really quite sad. A new shopping center was developed only seven blocks away at Central Avenue and Camelback. A new, larger hardware store run by L.L. Smith opened and dad couldn't compete. At that time the discount stores like GovWay and FedMart and KMart began to put lots of mom and pop businesses on the ropes. Dad's store was a victim of progress. He loved his store. It broke his heart to give up his dream. Eventually, he was hired to work as a mechanical draftsman on space exploration projects for Motorola Research where he worked for fifteen years up to the time of his retirement.

I went to work at a small Maytag store, a washing machine sales and service outfit run by an elderly man who did me the honor of firing me for the first and only time in my life. I was hired to do service work, mostly home service calls to repair automatic Maytag washing machines that had just come on the market to replace the old wringer-type machines. I went through company sponsored schooling to learn the skills.

I had complained to my boss several times that I thought the truck was unsafe to drive. He responded by sending me out on more service calls. I tried to express my concern again and he told me to stop bitchin' and do my job. One day I was driving down Baseline Road in south Phoenix when a young boy about ten or so ran out in front of the truck. I grabbed the wheel to keep the truck straight. I applied the brakes, locking all four wheels. The bald tires just slid on the smooth pavement. The truck popped out of gear and the left door flew open as I got the damned thing stopped with the young boy just under the front bumper! Miraculously, I hadn't touched him. He scampered away and was gone.

I drove back to the store immediately and told my boss what had happened. He fired me on the spot for driving recklessly! A few weeks later, after I went to work for a different Maytag business. I saw the old Studebaker, still on the road, still in terrible shape being driven by some other dude who was risking his own life and the lives of others. For thirty-eight years in the classroom I told each class about that guy who fired me and about that '51 Studebaker truck. I showed each class the Studebaker distributor rotor that I took with me when I left that day and carried in my briefcase for half a lifetime. I told my classes, "I hope that turkey is still looking for this thing." It always got a laugh.

Sharon wasn't quite the same after she came back from San Francisco. She said she still loved me, but I sensed that something was wrong. Finally one day, as we sat in my car during a lunch break from our jobs, she showed me the diamond ring that her Frisco fellow had sent her and told me she was gonna get married, presumably not to me. "Now," says I to me, "if she says she loves me, but is gonna marry him, there's a little something going on here." There sure was and that's exactly what she did.

I remember how Shirley helped me keep my head straight over the next few months. I was beginning to learn about real life. Mom said I would forget my Sharon's name in a year or two. She was wrong. You never forget that first crush, even though better things are almost sure to follow.

Things changed dramatically for me over the course of the next year. 1952 was the year I turned nineteen, the year that I left my childhood and became a young man.

Chapter Four

The Fighting Machine

Imagine my delight when I discovered that the mailbox contained a letter for me that bore the official seal of the President of the United States of America.

> *October 26, 1952*
>
> *Dear Mr. Donald Huard,*
>
> *Greetings from the Office of the President: You have been selected by a committee of your local peers to serve in the armed Services of the United States of America. You will be expected to appear at 201 N. First Avenue, Phoenix, Arizona at 07:00 A.M. on November 28, 1952 for induction into the United States Army.*
>
> *Sincerely yours,*
> *Dwight David Eisenhower*
> *President of the United States*

"I like Ike - I like Ike!" That's what the voters cheered at the political convention for the republicans in late 1951. The election that followed showed that a great many voters agreed with the slogan, enough to elect the former military general and national hero overwhelmingly over Adlai Stevenson, the popular Governor of Illinois. As Eisenhower's predecessor, Harry Truman, had lost much of his popularity as the democratic president during the latter part of his term because of his decision to support the South Koreans against invasion from the north across the 38th parallel in the Korean Peninsula.

Later in the war, Truman fired the popular General Douglas McArthur who wanted to invade the north and also China to punish the communists for their transgressions. This further eroded his presidential popularity. Eisenhower, on the other hand, had no popularity problems, that is, except with young Donnie Huard who didn't particularly like his mailing habits.

I had just turned eighteen in May of that year, was still working for a kindly, considerate boss at the Maytag Store and was still hurting, feeling romantically disadvantaged. Then came the Asian flu. My boss sent me home for a few days to heave and weave. That became two weeks of self-pity and weight loss. When I "checked in" for active military duty a few weeks later I looked like I had just been released from a WWII prison camp. I weighed 115 lbs!

Dad took me down to the recruiting station that unhappy morning for my induction. On the way there, he told me not to let my mind get too far away from home and those who loved me. Dad could be surprisingly sentimental at times. I remember, when I was inside the building after having said goodbye, I looked out through the window and saw dad with his forehead leaning downward against the top of the Chevy steering wheel. His sons had survived the big war. And then came the Korean War. We both wondered what was ahead. For me, it was a bus ride to Fort Ord, California near San Francisco.

From that 07:00 A.M. on November 28, 1952 until 02:00 P.M. on November 27, 1954 I maintained a most remarkable hate relationship with anything and everything military. I looked like Ichabod Crane in my uniform. They yanked my front teeth. Everyone else was twice as strong as I was and (I thought) half as scared as I was. Nobody was more homesick than I was.

There I was, fifty pounds lighter than the others, so skinny I could almost hide behind my rifle, trying to act like a big tough dude, a real mean fighting machine… I'm sure any North Korean soldier confronted by me would have been terrified.

As you might guess, they don't have a lot of patience with frail mamma's boys when you're in basic training. So I got yelled at more than most of the others, picked on more than the others and did more KP duty than the others, but I did the best that I could and apparently it was good enough. I learned to clown a bit. If any big 200 pounder got on my tail and gave me any lip I would loudly tell him I was gonna kick his ass and I would dance and jab at the air while everyone laughed. My own left hook was so vicious it nearly knocked *me* off my feet. Whew! Survived another one…

Surprisingly, especially to myself, I began to toughen up. After two weeks or so I began to think that I might actually get through basic training alive! The calisthenics were grueling. That M-1 rifle was a lot heavier for me than it was for the other guys. They should have gotten me another BB gun. It seemed as though we ran all day long. We ran to chow, to the rifle range, to the infiltration course, to the latrine. I wondered at that time why the army needed so many trucks. They sure didn't use them. I never knew that my feet could hurt so much.

On the rifle range I did quite well. I fired sharpshooter with the M-1 rifle. Nine rounds then "PING," out would fly the empty clip. Stuff another one in while keeping your thumb clear and fire away again. Each raw recruit got his thumb caught in the breech of that weapon only once. It was a lesson learned quickly and completely with only one trial.

I did better with the M-1 carbine, a short cartridge .30 caliber rifle often used for closer combat. It was lighter. I could handle it better and I actually got an X-pert marksmanship medal for my performance. Then there was the heavier Browning automatic rifle (B A R) that could be 'fanned" to fire only a single round in order to fool the enemy into thinking that it was only an M-1 rifle. Then we went to mortars and learned how to drop round after round into a thirty foot radius using a method called bracketing.

During the first days of basic training, the recruit's world becomes one of disorientation, confusion and pain. It was never like this at home.

Mom used to wake me up in the mid-morning by gently calling me or nudging my lazy bones. At Fort Ord the cadre walked into the barracks at 04:00 A.M. and dropped a grenade simulator into an empty garbage can. I went from prone to panic in a nanosecond.

Fighting on the bayonet course, firing on the rifle ranges and running the rest of each day left us all exhausted by 11:00 P.M. bedtime. I would lay in the dark listening to the snoring of others that sounded like mine does today, trying not to go to sleep because I knew that in an instant that grenade would go off, giving new meaning to the Big Bang Theory.

As a survival mechanism I developed a little technique. I would lay on my back thinking about the events of the day, trying to process my head until I felt a little more in contact with reality, then flip over onto my stomach and enjoy five hours of blissful splendor before Sergeant macho came in to very "gently" awaken me. The lasting effect of this is that even now I cannot go to sleep on my back. If I stay on my back I will stay awake. Since I am old now, however, when I flip to my stomach I will still lay awake.

A buddy of mine had another trick that helped him deal with the discomforts and miseries of military life. He talked the fellows at the supply window to issue him combat boots that were two sizes too small. On the rifle range and on the long marches he would groan and agonize over the condition of his feet. Yet, he still wore those boots every day. We tried to tell him to get bigger boots. "Look," he would say, "I got drafted and here I am. The sergeant is on my ass all of the time. I keep busting my thumb in that damn rifle. My dog got killed by a bus. My wife is divorcing me. The only time I feel good is when I take off these effin' boots!"

All recruits were gathered into a huge set of bleachers one day to witness a demonstration of the firing of a most remarkable weapon. Called a recoilless rifle, this 57 millimeter "canon" was resting on a tripod about twenty yards just in front of us. That artillery piece was amazingly powerful for something small enough to be fired from the shoulder. The cadre (usually the high ranking corporals) gave us a memorable demonstration.

The back breech of the weapon is open, resulting in a back blast that counters the muzzle pressure that propels a high explosive anti-tank shell that can be placed accurately on target at 2,000 yards! When the gun goes off there is no recoil whatever. Because of the open breech the sound of that thing going off is deafening.

When it was time for a raw, dumb recruit to fire it, guess who got picked from the crowd? On rubbery knees, I got next to that thing and waited just as instructed until Corporal Bravo loaded the charge. "Just like with the M-1, take a deep breath, sight in that old tank out there, exhale slowly with your mouth open and squeeze the trigger," I was told. Well, there's always that ten percent who don't get the word. I forgot the open the mouth part. When that damned thing went off I thought the charge had hit my head. It was like a 747 jet with a flaming afterburner was flying in my right inner ear.

I turned to the corporal I couldn't hear and saw him shaking his fist at me as he kicked at me, chasing me back into the bleachers. Apparently, the safest place to be was in the tank I was shooting at. I missed the target by over fifty yards! The reason you keep your mouth open is because some of the air pressure can enter the throat and the Eustachian tube to the middle ear to counter the pressure on the external eardrum when the blast occurs. I didn't. And it didn't. So I sustained a broken eardrum!

I worked amidst the jet airplanes doing KP duty in the chow hall the next day and couldn't hear the metal trays crashing against the metal countertops. Those were the days when a broken eardrum meant you got aspirin tablets from the infirmary. Today, the recruit would get a medical discharge, go on disability and be supported by Uncle Sam forever. I went on to a few more days of policing the kitchen in high pitched ecstasy before returning to my regular duties on the infiltration course. My hearing is still a bit weak on the right side. Happily, that's the side my wife is on when I'm driving.

Just prior to my entering the Army I began to date the girl who lived across the street from my parents' home. Kathy was a very fine young lady of seventeen or so when we met. When I went off to Fort Ord she wrote me often and helped to keep my spirits up as I endured that awful loneliness of being away from home.

Only one month into basic training a few of us got the idea of pooling our meager finances and chartering a light airplane out of nearby Monterey, California to fly us to Phoenix for a very short Christmas weekend. We had only a 48-hour pass, so we were not authorized to go any farther than Los Angeles.

However, we figured that once we got off the base, Corporals Macho and Bravo would have no idea what we were up to or where we went as long as we got back in time. A hippie-looking pilot and five Phoenix soldiers crowded into the vintage twin engine Cessna and hung on for dear life.

The old twin radial engines were so noisy it was almost unbearable. We were clearly overloaded. There were only four seats so two of us sat on the floor for the entire flight. In spite of the inconveniences, we had a great break from the miseries of basic training. I was able to spend Christmas at home, probably the best Christmas I ever experienced. Mom stuffed me with her very special chop suey over mashed potatoes, rice raisin pudding and lemon meringue pie.

Kathy and her uniformed adolescent went out on a special date. I brought her home a little late and her parents didn't complain. The next morning dad, mom and Kathy went to the airport with me to see us take off for our reluctant return to the fun and games of military life. Kathy continued writing to me, letters that I waited for all through my two years in the service. We dated whenever I got back home and even for a year or so after I got out. She encouraged me to go to college with her at Phoenix College. I'm not sure whether Kathy and I were ever really in love, but we were surely sweethearts and cared a great deal for each other. My memories of that sweet girl remain special to this day.

The Korean police action ranged on as my two months of basic training progressed. Tests were given to determine if we were good candidates for special schools like the officer candidate school, clerk typist school, dental technician school or paramedic school, etc. I flunked them all. Any fellow who had bombed his way through high school, as I had, was learning deficient, a poor prospect for anything other than two more months of infantry training. So, I climbed taller hills, carried bigger weapons, crawled longer infiltration courses under "enemy" machine gunfire and learned how to "dig in" to escape from a barrage of incoming artillery. As my training neared its end I began to resign myself to the idea that I would be sent to Korea as a foot soldier to apply my new skills, none of which I had ever asked for and all of which I despised.

Then came one of the proudest days of my life. On a huge open parade ground covered with plush green grass, Company B of the First Infantry Regiment passed in review before a crowd of officers and family members as graduates of the Fort Ord Basic Training Program. And right in the middle of those perfectly aligned rows of disciplined soldiers marched Donald Huard, in full dress uniform with "Ike" jacket and blue trim, rifle angled just right, snapping his head right on command as he passed the reviewing stand just like in the movies.

I had made it. Now I was part of that fighting machine. Not bad for a 115 pound kid who, six months earlier, was afraid of being away from home, afraid to go to sleep at night, afraid of the sound of weapons, afraid of life. Master Sergeant Willy Jenkens, a huge black man with the most powerful voice I had ever heard, yelled the perfect cadence above the sound of the marching band that day, one of the best days of my life.

Sure enough, my first orders were for FECOM. That meant Far East Command. That meant Korea. First, however, eight glorious days on leave, back in Phoenix, Arizona with the sweet smell of orange blossoms, mom's macaroni and tomato soup, more chop suey over mashed potatoes, the drive-in movies with Kathy and sleeping in until 10 o'clock in the mornings before mom gently "nudged" me awake for TV and breakfast.

I didn't tell mom and dad right away where I was going. I just didn't want to talk about it for awhile. When it was time to leave, I told them what they already knew.

Looking back on it now, I have to admit that basic training in the Army was good for me. I was shaken from my sad feelings of self-pity over losing my sweetheart a few months earlier. I learned in a hurry what a great family life I had and how much mom and dad catered to their children. I was forced to accept rigid discipline that bordered on the ridiculous with inspections by officers I learned to fear but came to respect.

I learned how welcome a letter from home could be. Most of all, having met my responsibility to survive and produce, I was on the way to developing some self-confidence and a feeling that, after all, there was some hope for the skinny kid from Phoenix.

When I finished my sixteen weeks of light and heavy weapons infantry basic training I didn't know what the future would hold for me. Would I be sent to actually fight in the war? Was it really a war at all? Many referred to the Korean conflict as a police action, undeclared as a war. Nonetheless, I could be asked to kill others or even to die for my country.

Still, I was proud of my achievement of mere survival of the training. Not bad for one who was so frail as a raw recruit, one pulled away from home at such an early age, one who had to prove himself capable of becoming a disciplined soldier ready to handle a soldier's potential challenges.

I felt a little more confident about myself after my basic training, feeling that, after all, there just might be some hope for the 115 lb. Private Donald Huard, a graduate infantryman in Company B of the 6th Division of the United States Army.

The Fighting Machine

With buddy Dave,
seasick for five days
aboard the
USS JEFFERSON
bound for Alaska
1953

Chapter Five

From Wheels to Wings

My own fascination with motors, motorbikes and automobiles and my natural affinity for wallowing in oil and grease may have left me unpalatable for some of my girlfriends' parents, but it did serve a useful purpose. It made me into a reasonably good mechanic. Late in my teens I began to pride myself in the fact that I could make any gas-powered lawnmower purr like a new one and any auto engine run, long after it was abandoned by others.

My Rollfast bike didn't have a motor, but soon, at age fifteen, I was the proud owner of a *Springcycle*, a primitive bicycle with a flexible platform that held a Clinton 2.3 horse power gasoline engine. I was forever cleaning the old spark plug, grinding the valves and tinkering on the carburetor on that thing even when it didn't need any tuning whatever.

Soon I graduated up to a Cushman Scooter with its massive 4 horsepower engine and room enough on the back for one passenger. I learned quickly how to fix a kick starter, replace a head gasket, rough up the bands in the centrifugal clutch and adjust the ignition breaker points to get maximum performance. I loved tinkering on anything that had a motor.

One day as Sharon and I walked home hand in hand from North Phoenix High School, I noticed a man trying to get the engine started on a cute little solid black 1932 Chevy Two-door Sedan sitting on the driveway next to his house. He had an engine crank in his hand with one end stuffed through the radiator into the front of the engine. Guess who was soon holding the gas pedal down slightly and adjusting the choke while he turned the engine over. When the engine turned on, my soul ignited with it.

The fellow told me that he was gonna sell the car, but couldn't because the Bendix spring in the starter had broken and he didn't have the money to replace it. "How much do you want for this car," I asked? "Well," he answered, "Sure am tired of cranking it to start it. If I could get $60 for it I'd be happy."

Dad told me at the hardware store that it sounded good to him, but all that I needed was $60 to buy it. Now, dads are supposed to lay out the cash for a kid for his first set of real wheels today, but in those days you were more likely to find "Pop" a little less compliant. "Where are *you* gonna get $60," he asked? I would have scrubbed the streets of Phoenix on my hands and knees to get my wrenches on that car.

I sold my scooter for $22, washed cars on Saturdays across the street from the store at Norm Stayeart's Standard Gas Station, worked on mom and dad for a loan for the difference and made the deal for that sucker, the deal of a lifetime! My wrist was sore all of the time form cranking that engine. I didn't mind it a bit. Sixteen and licensed, I was everywhere with that car. I could fix flat tires, tune the distributor that didn't need tuning, advance and retard the spark. You name it, I could do it. I polished the black paint to make it glisten in the sun. Then I polished the glistening paint again. Then I really spiffied it up for any date with my girlfriend. I fixed the starter, adjusted the old mechanical brakes and changed the oil more frequently than the oil in my own hair.

I couldn't stop it in time one afternoon and plowed into the back of a big truck giving my chrome radiator cover the cutest pug nose. I put a fancy necker's knob on the steering wheel to free up my right arm to go around my sweetie as *she* shifted the gears. Were those the good ole' days? Yeah! Yeah! Oh, Yeah!

It's too bad that when we're having the good ole' days we're too young to know that those are the good ole' days. It's too bad that when we're young we feel so oppressed by life that we fail to recognize how little is being asked of us and how much we have, without really having to pay for it ourselves. Being the typical kid, I thought life was tough then, well before I had any real responsibilities or had to pay any prices for having it so good. I was not inclined to fully appreciate the fact that my parents were the one's carrying the burdens for me, letting me enjoy life without the intrusion of responsible reality.

I never assumed it was a problem, but it was a fact that I liked driving my Chevy a little hot. Well, no, it's more like I drove it *very* hot! If you want to know the honest truth, I drove it like a race car and proceeded to beat the stuffings out of it. Soon it wasn't anything like the polished black beauty I was so proud of. With a few crunched fenders, a pug-nosed grille and a twisted rear bumper, it was just like any other old junk car.

My big brother Ray rescued me at about that time. He had a really neat green 1933 Plymouth Sedan that he drove sanely, one he was considering trading in on a brand new 1952 Chevy Coupe. Both my Chevy and his Plymouth were quite old by then so neither was worth very much. Ray volunteered to give me his Plymouth and trade my Chevy in on his new car. The result was that I got a real clean, solid sedan with a newly rebuilt engine which I also proceeded to beat the stuffings out of, just as I had done to the Chevy.

I just couldn't keep my foot out of the carburetors of any car I owned. I would wind the engines too tight, speed shift the vehicles into second gear to make the tires "bark" on the pavement, drag race anyone who would accept a challenge and endanger the lives of anyone in my way.

Dad told me that I shouldn't buy that big blue 1942 Hudson Sedan with the Hydramatic transmission that I saw on a used car lot on Van Buren Street. It was priced at $495, which was too much for me. "Look at this neat little '38 Ford Coupe that is just right for you at $185," he advised. I wouldn't listen to him, of course, so I bought the Hudson and blew the transmission within three short months. I took that huge transmission out of the car myself in the backyard on Meadowbrook, hauled it over to the dealer to get it reworked, reinstalled it, then blew it again. Eventually, I broke a piston in the engine by winding it to the max and I sold the car for almost nothing. Dad didn't say much. That '38 Ford was sure in nice shape…

I bought and sold many a used car before the days when I found myself running up and down the hills of Fort Ord, California, carrying machine guns and mortars. There was no use to have a car when I was in basic training. I had to live in the barracks and was confined like a slave. There was no use to have a car if I was gonna freeze my tail off in the hills of Korea.

So I returned from my glorious eight day leave in Phoenix to a military base in the Presidio of San Francisco as instructed on my orders. I stayed away just about as long as I could get away with. If I had waited until any time after midnight that Sunday night I would have been A.W.O.L. Just an hour before the deadline I checked in. The new sergeant checked to find my name on his guest list then said, "It's going to be cold where you're going." I said, "Yes, Sir, I know…" I must have had the look of the doomed on my face. "It's really cold in Alaska," he said. "ALASKA," I yelled. "Oh, you're another one who didn't get the word. Your orders have been changed," he said. "You're not going to Korea."

I worked my way through dozens of other excited soldiers all trying to get to a telephone to call home to break the good news. "I'm going to ALASKA," I screamed at mom and dad in the middle of the night. Sure enough, in a few days I was aboard the U.S.S. Jefferson, a rusty WWII troop ship headed for an incredible adventure amidst the glaciers and the Eskimos.

As it turned out, while we were all on leave with our orders for Korea, a general somewhere needed a company of GIs to serve as a supply unit for a private company contracted to survey large parts of Alaska preparatory to its becoming America's next state. The company was called the Coastal Geodetic Survey Company and our infantry regiment was linked to the 30th Engineer's Base Topographical Battalion. We were assigned as a support unit for the surveyors. From then on we all wore the castle-like *Imprimus* Army Engineer patches on our Ike jackets.

A little background material about the history of the Alaskan Peninsula can be helpful at this point. Alaska occupies the most northwestern portion of the North American Continent. Farther west, across the fifty-one miles of the Bering Strait is the Cukotsku Peninsula of the Soviet Union. During the 1800s, Alaska was called Russian America before the United States bought the rights to the area from Russia for a negotiated purchase price of $7.3 million, about 8 cents per acre. The transfer of Alaska to the U.S. occurred just after the Civil War in 1867. It remained a U.S. Territory for the remainder of the century and up through the Second World War. In 1953, young Don Huard arrived to help survey the land, resulting in the acceptance by President Eisenhower of Alaska in 1959 as the 49th American State.

The five-day trip aboard the U.S.S. Jefferson was fine for about one-half of the first day at sea. On the second day I began to yearn for the hills of Korea. Never before (or since, for that matter) have I ever been so cold, sick and incapacitated. I learned very quickly that a ship at sea does not simply float in a straight line to its destination. Instead, it sways its way from side to side, nose going up and down, its passengers getting sicker and sicker with each creak and groan of the ancient timbers strung together in its belly. I heaved for four of the five days. For four horrible days that seemed like a month, I lay in the hold of that torture pit, praying that I wouldn't fall off of the floor.

Twice a day we were forced out of the hold, up on deck to "enjoy" (heave into) the sea. Because the ship was swaying from side to side in the rough sea, when we stood looking to the left or right on a natural parallel line with the deck we could see an alternating wall of water rushing toward us at one moment, then a wall of sky the next. The water looked as though it would wash us overboard, but it didn't. Anyway, we were all too sick to care.

Late in the afternoon of the fifth day the water began to smooth out. Huge Glaciers appeared near the shoreline of the Cook Inlet that narrowed its way toward the Alaskan city of Anchorage. The scenery was absolutely incredible. Bolstered by the thought that I might actually get off of that bolt bucket and inspired by what I had never dreamed my eyes would see, I clicked away with my cheap box camera loaded with black and white film.

Dave, a Kentucky born friend with an enormous southern drawl, was kind enough to carry my duffle bag off of the ship for me. I was too weak to do it myself. A few hours later we were on a train that slowly climbed through the beautiful snow-covered mountains. Then, we were loaded on trucks for transport to Fort Richardson, an army installation on the outskirts of Anchorage.

A few days later I found myself strapped to a jump seat mounted against the inner wall of a huge C-130 Cargo Transport plane with forty other soldiers who, along with three Hiller H-23 helicopters, were being sent to a small airstrip at Galena. It was a miniature outpost in a remote area on the Yukon River in central Alaska.

There we would serve through the summer months as support staff for the Coastal Geodetic Surveyors. My specific responsibility became clear in short order. I was given an airplane, a Cessna 180, and told to keep it in shape to fly. I had never even been in a small airplane before, let alone been expected to serve as a maintenance specialist for one of them. I knew that the propeller was on the front end and the stick made it go up and down.

Out of the innards of a Beechcraft Bonanza one day stepped a short young man of twenty-three or so, the man who was to be my pilot on the L-19 Birddog I was assigned to maintain. He looked a little like me, weighing in at about 125 lbs. However, he was only about 5'3" tall. The difference was that he proudly carried First Lieutenant's bars on his shoulders and by me he was called "Sir."

I liked my new lieutenant pilot boss right from the start. He could have turned out to be a real nerd. But he didn't. He could have been overly bossy. But he wasn't. He turned out to be a nice kid with lots of smarts, a competent, friendly personality and, most important of all, he was a natural as a bush pilot. We risked our necks together in that airplane sometimes that summer and I always felt confident in his ability to get us safely back on the runway. Except for once. I think that we made a pretty good team.

All around our "home base" of Galena, with its 10,000 foot runway suitable for landing jet fighters and cargo planes, there were small surveyor camps with men living in tents heated with oil stoves. The camps were on high plateaus or next to river beds or in dirt clearings from which small helicopters transported crews to remote areas to do their work. Our job with the Birddog was to keep the 'copters supplied with fuel and parts, the crews supplied with food, water and the ever-important mail from home. To do this, we took off and landed, often at considerable peril, from very short, very rough runways carved in the wilderness.

My little lieutenant became extremely skilled at "plopping" our overloaded L-19 onto a cleared runway and getting it stopped just before we hit the trees or went for a swim. We were in and out of camps at places called Kaltag, Nulatto, Ruby (the hotspot for Klondike Kate during the late 1800s Gold Rush Days) and McGrath. At the end of each day we returned to the long, smooth runway at Galena and the Quonset huts used for our barracks away from home.

We considered ourselves lucky to be in those Quonset huts rather than in tents. At least they had some solid walls and a little insulation against the cold. At least we were near the "town," a community that had a population of, say, twenty elderly Eskimos, a dozen Huskie dogs and a small post office. There were no young people, no pretty girls in brightly colored dresses, no Burger King Restaurants for us along the Yukon. Just military olive drab and more military olive drab. And loneliness for our girlfriends and our families.

In the midst of winter there is little daylight in Alaska, maybe only several hours each day. In midsummer there is very little darkness. We had arrived in Galena in mid-April when the long winter nights were about over and the weather was warming a bit. The mosquito population was in the zillions requiring us to work on our planes wearing head nets and gloves. It became difficult to sleep during June and July when there was little darkness. Our work days grew longer as the weeks went by, as the crews were under pressure to do as much surveying as possible before the next winter set in and we reluctantly (?) had to return to San Francisco.

The pressures of bush flying over extremely rugged terrain, getting in and out of dangerous airstrips amidst trees and on sandbars left pilots and crews exhausted at day's end. So much so that late in the afternoon of one August day my pilot fell asleep at the stick while making a landing at Galena!

Sitting in the back of the plane as we approached the runway, I noticed that we seemed a little too high for our usual landing approach. I then noticed a few of the helicopter mechanics down on the deck as they began to wave frantically at us, trying to warn us, "You're too high. You're too high!"

I slammed my hand against the back of the pilot's seat. When the lieutenant came to the realization that he had landed on the wrong end of the runway, going in the wrong direction and was going off of the end into a deep ravine, he awakened in a hurry. It was too late. So much for U.S. Army 2825, one L-19 Birddog that never flew again. And I never flew with the young lieutenant after that. I don't know what ever happened to him.

A helicopter pilot and a crew chief, who was a friend of mine, were killed that summer when for some unknown reason the main rotor blade of their copter came off in flight. They didn't stand a chance of survival. I did a little more growing up that day as I helped to carry the bodies in blood-soaked blankets for loading onto a Navy SA-16 amphibious plane for transport back to Anchorage. I remember my first sergeant saying to me, "It's all part of life, kid. It's all part of life." It was a part I had not seen until then.

In October, as the days grew short again, we and the 'copters were loaded back into the C-130s and shipped back to Anchorage. Within days we were afloat again for our five-day, not quite so seasick trip back to one of the most beautiful sights that a homesick American soldier can ever feast his eyes on, the image, looming larger and larger the closer you get, of the San Francisco Golden Gate Bridge.

At the base of that bridge is the Presidio of California. Fort Winfield Scott is located there and there is a small airstrip used by the Aviation Detachment of the 30th Engineer's Base Topographical Battalion. It wasn't Phoenix. It wasn't chop suey over mashed potatoes. But, it meant cable cars and movie theaters. It meant young girls in pretty dresses. It meant relief from olive drab. It meant the end of another chapter, a time in my life when I was establishing a bit of independence from my family while on an adventure that could happen only once in a lifetime, or so I thought. Little did I know at the time that I was to spend a second tour the following year assigned more aircraft maintenance responsibility in the same little village of Galena, just next to the Yukon River.

On sometimes dangerous trips to the remote areas being surveyed I usually carried a side-arm .45 Colt semi-automatic pistol meant for protection should our airplane go down in a survivable crash. I couldn't hit anything with it but I felt more secure against the huge bears roaming in the wild amidst all kinds of smaller animals. Imagining myself stranded at night, in the cold waiting for the sound of a rescue helicopter, I came to understand why I was being paid several bucks extra per month as hazardous duty pay. "Maybe," I thought, "I might have been safer in Korea, after all."

Grandpa Don was drafted into the U.S. Army by President Eisenhower in 1952. After sixteen weeks of light and heavy weapons training, his orders to serve in Korea were changed. Don was assigned to the 30th Engineers Topographical Battalion and sent to San Marcos, Texas to the Kelly Air Force Base for training in fixed-wing aircraft maintenance. He served out his military term as a crew-chief on the DeHavilland "Beaver" in the Yukon Territory in Central Alaska.

-- 1952-54 --

Following his military service, Don attended Phoenix Community College and earned four degrees at a University including a Ph.D. in research psychology.

Chapter Six

Beaver Love...

At last, the army was going to teach me how to work on airplanes, well after I had been doing so for the last six months, risking my own neck and that of my pilot as well. They took me from the comfort of my home in Phoenix when I was just a boy, beat the hell out of me for six months, sent me to that place so cold my fingers would crack, then assigned me an airplane and said "Fix it." There's much to the oft-spoken words "There's the right way and then there's the army way."

I have to admit, it was better by far than Korea. Even safer than Korea, in spite of my lack of skills. It was my familiarity with grease, oil, spark plugs, filters, wheel bearings, carburetors and busted knuckles that saved me. Most of the time I learned by doing things accidentally right. Sometimes, I did actually know what I was doing. We survived the summer quite well except for the price of one airplane that was destroyed by someone else's error. That poor young lieutenant!

My next orders, fulfilled through the winter of 1953-54, were for transfer to the Kelly Air Force Base in San Marcos, Texas to be trained as a fixed-wing aircraft frame and engine mechanic. It was nice and warm there. I learned how to prop-start an L-16 without losing my head, just like cranking the old Chevy, except that you had to duck. I *did* follow directions that time.

The schooling took about eight weeks, during which time much of what I was learning was just old hat to a veteran pro. Some of it, however, was quite fascinating. I learned about magnetos, engine breakdown and reassembly. I learned a lot about fuel systems and the problems pilots faced when they had to fly at higher altitudes to clear mountain terrain. We learned about survival techniques in case we went down and had to be located either during the day or at night. We learned about parachutes and I learned how to pray.

There was absolutely nothing interesting about San Marcos itself. We were confined to the base except for weekends, then encouraged to stay out of any of the local night spots, many of which had signs on the doors, "Soldiers and Dogs Keep Out." I did my job, learned as much as I could, stayed out of any major trouble and looked forward to the trip back to San Francisco as it meant a few days in Phoenix on the way.

In Phoenix, I visited with family, dated Kathy, visited with her folks (whom I liked) and spent a couple of days hunting for a used car to take back to the base. I ended up with a 1950 Olds 88 Sedan that was sharp and hot and two-tone blue.

Out of basic training and with a little more freedom in San Francisco, I began to make some friends, notably because I was the one who had a nice car. Although painfully shy about "foreign" girls, I double-dated a few times and became familiar with the young party set. I was, however, never comfortable with a drink in my hand. I seemed relaxed only when I was working on my L-19 or my Olds, never when socializing with the "with it" crowd.

Then, there was the shape-up program sponsored by some macho colonel who was trying to impress some general with the spit and polish of his troops. We stood at attention in the barracks for endless stupid inspections and military discipline. I hated that nonsense with a passion. It was too much like going to confession. Besides, one smart-assed captain actually asked me if I had stolen my uniform because it was too big for me. Those Ike jackets only came so small and, remember, I was a very skinny kid.

As winter turned to spring, plans were again being made for more summer surveying with the Coastal Geodetic Group. We did special inspections on our aircraft preparing them for the heavy work ahead. One day, Moriarty called me into the maintenance office and told me that I had been selected to be a crew-chief on a larger plane. A

DeHaviland Beaver, called the Army L-20. Furthermore, said my boss, you are going to be one of the fellows who will fly in the plane to Alaska, then on to Galena.

That meant several things to me. One was that I had earned a step up in responsibility by doing a good job on the L-19. The second was that I would have an assistant to boss around (he was an Italian kid most helpful - a funny, funny guy who laughed like that donkey in Memphis) and third, that I would not have to spend five days up and five days back desperately seasick on the U.S.S. Boltbucket!

That L-20 was something else! Man, how I learned to love that airplane! However, the army did it to me again. Having been trained belatedly on how to take care of a small Cessna L-19 that I had already worked on for six full months, the brass sent me back to Galena to work on a different kind of airplane with no training on it either. While the L-19 was a tandem two-seater with the pilot up front and the passenger behind him, powered by a 180 horse power six cylinder opposed Continental engine, the "Beaver" was a six passenger plane with a nine cylinder 450 horsepower Pratt Whitney Radial engine. It was supercharged - and so was I!

Now, I've been saying that I hated the army, that I had a remarkable hate relationship with anything and everything military. That airplane was the exception to the rule. To this day, I adore that airplane. I have actually considered getting a license to fly and buying one of those airplanes! Obviously, I'm going to have much to say about that airplane.

The Beaver is a boxy looking, squarish looking plane, round only at the front cowling over its great big engine. Mine was white with red trim with U.S. Army 2813 painted on its rudder and "Lucky Thirteen" on its nose. The interior of the airplane was wide enough for me to sit crew-chief co-pilot on our flights next to one of the neatest people I ever knew, my pilot, Captain Paul Hopkins. There were four seats behind us used for traveling brass or other personnel. We could remove those seats and make the plane into a cargo carrier. It was the perfect vehicle for short strip take-offs and landings. Many of the used ones are being used today in jungles or with floats on lakes and rivers all over the world.

Harrison Ford even crashed a Beaver in one of his recent movies. His co-star Ann Hecht wanted him to "glue" it back together.

Riding in one, behind the roar of that radial engine, is a real adventure. The engine has what is called an "inertia" starter. What that means is that unlike an automobile that has its starter connected directly to the engine, the plane uses a battery to energize a heavy flywheel that whines louder and louder, increasing in RPMs until it is suddenly engaged so that the heavy weight of the spinning wheel can crank the engine. If you are lucky, it starts with a monstrous roar.

Radial engines run notoriously rough when they first start and are at low RPMs. The airframe shakes, the engine sputters, backfires and chokes on the full rich mixture of fuel needed to get it running. When the throttle is advanced slowly and the mixture is leaned, the power becomes smooth at about 1000 RPMs and as a motor-lovin' kid from Phoenix I would go into orbit each time. I was absolutely enthralled by the power. It was like being on a set of rails at the local drag strip. I nearly peed with excitement whenever we took that thing off.

In early April of 1954 I sat in the back of Lucky Thirteen behind a couple of very capable military pilots as we took off on the first leg of a most exciting trip up through Canada, the Yukon Territory and into Alaska. The first stop was in Elko, Nevada. We stayed overnight in a hotel and were treated to a fabulous meal as though we were royal guests.

The next day we flew to Butte, Montana where we landed in a fifty mile an hour crosswind. It took repeated attempts before we could get glued to the runway. Each time we were about to touch down, a gust of wind would lift us up and throw us to the right or left. A wise captain used a clever technique I had seen my L-19 pilot use in the mountains. He intentionally came in with the flaps down, waiting until just the right time to yank up on the lever and take all of the flight out of the aircraft. We essentially crashed the plane in and prayed that we would stay down on the runway. It worked. I, of course, was not nervous at all, being the veteran crew-chief that I was.

From Butte, it was into Canada with our next stop at Calgary, then on to Edmonton, Alberta where another hotel stay was made interesting by the activity of our officers in the room next to us, having what sounded like a very fine time with a few very noisy women. One of the perks of Officers' Candidate School, I guess. Enlisted men, of course, were not included.

We flew seven airplanes in squadron type formations, two of the larger Beavers and five L19s with pilots radioing back and forth as we cruised over the green rolling hills of western Alberta. The air was smooth, the scenery inspiring, surely this was a better way to travel than my floor-clinging naval adventure of a year earlier.

We landed next at Dawson Creek, a very small outpost with an aviation fuel station, a few villagers and just about nothing else. It was getting colder the farther north we went and we seemed to get farther and farther from civilization. Another day's flying brought us to White Horse in the Yukon Territory where we got weathered in for a few extra days.

The first night we were there, several of us went to the little local bar and listened to the noisy jukebox music and watched as a few of the younger residents danced.

One young girl sat all alone at one of the tables, looking somewhat dejected and tearful. My buddy and I went over and sat with her for awhile and let her tell her sad troubles to a couple of strange soldiers. Later, as we walked to our temporary quarters in the dark, we were accosted by a few of the local boys who apparently resented our attentions to the young girl. They called us "Yanks" and tried to start a rumble, but decided against it when they saw how big I was… And how there were about a dozen or so other Yanks in the area.

After a short fuel stop at St. John, then another at Dawson before leaving the Yukon Territory, we entered Alaska, stopping at Northway. Then, climbing over some very treacherous mountains we settled into Anchorage. It was a splendid adventure for a skinny kid from the desert. I was quite proud to be a crew-chief on one of the bigger planes, one of the supercharged and radial-engine planes, one with a variable-pitch prop and the sound of a DC-3. A few days' rest, then we headed for my old stompin' grounds at Galena.

Flying from Anchorage to Galena involved risking our lives when we traveled in aircraft light enough to be thrown this way and that by the buffeting air currents naturally produced by winds ricocheting off of majestic mountains. Our only stop in between was at McGrath. To get to that location we had to climb to over 10,000 feet and go through a mountain pass next to Mt. McKinley that had become famous among Alaskan bush pilots for a tendency to gobble up light aircraft. We actually saw the wreckage of several that had not made it through that narrow passageway. Our anxiety levels increased to the point of nausea. I began to vomit. I was not the only one.

At that level, a light non-pressurized airplane is near its flying ceiling. The laboring engines, notably on the nonsupercharged L-19s were starved for oxygen, some of them overheating even in the frigid cold. The scenery was spectacular. Even that word -spectacular- could not describe the wonder and beauty before our eyes as we passed within a few thousand yards of the peak of Mt. McKinley. I felt as John Glenn must have felt when he was on his orbital space flight around the earth in 1962, as though I was sharing the wonders of creation in the presence of God.

Once through the pass and into some smoother air, I wrote a long letter to my sister Shirley. I had to share that experience with someone and I missed my big sister so much. Any fellow who didn't have a big sister while he was growing up, missed someone special. Shirley added balance to my life. And she still does. I left my Oldsmobile with her in Los Angeles before I headed north again, thinking that she would be pleased to have a car to drive while I was gone. It wasn't a good move, however, because it was not an easy starting car and she had so much trouble with it that it just sat unused most of the time.

Galena was, well, what can I say, just Galena. It wasn't a tourist's town by any measure. Just like the year before, it was too cold, then too hot, too humid, too dark, then too bright, and terribly lonely. Again I craved anything that had color to it. Except for the red and white of our airplanes, everything else was drab, the runway, the thousands of fifty-five gallon gasoline and oil drums, the empty hangers, the boredom, the waiting for letters from home...

I remember one day in mid-summer when a commercial airliner stopped at our airstrip to refuel. A door opened and for a magnificent half-hour a lovely lady stewardess in a plum-colored uniform stood on the ramp at the top of the stairs. Fueling the Beaver, one hundred yards away, I couldn't stop looking at her. "What in the hell am I doing here in drabsville," I asked? The vision of her made me even more lonely for the colors, the sweet smell of Kathy's cologne and the orange blossoms at home.

But there was work to be done. My portion of it was to keep that Beaver in operating condition, keep my capable pilot safe and happy and to help with the difficult task of supplying the helicopter crews and surveyors with many things they needed to do *their* jobs. So we were soon on our daily routines, mine involving the servicing, fueling and warming up of the engine and loading and belting in of nervous passengers or anchoring down cargo before my pilot would arrive for the flight. Sometimes I would go along, sometimes not.

My considerate pilot became a special friend, a mentor. He was a second "dad" to me for most of the remaining eight months I served in the military. He commanded more respect from the enlisted men there than the others, even some of higher rank, and I couldn't say exactly why. There was something about him, something about his strong confident personality and his natural control over even the most critical situations that gained respect from the men who worked with him.

The captain was a reserve officer, called back into the service during the Korean War after having served as a pilot in Europe in WWII. He was in his late thirties, a tall, striking-looking man who usually appeared neater than a hard day's flying should permit. He had a partial gold front tooth that added a little class to his look, a clear, strong voice that was gentle, unless he got mad. Then, look out! I heard him chew out a few recruits from time to time and he was a pro. Yet, in spite of a few times when he perhaps should have, he never came down on me. I think he knew how hard I was trying. Perhaps he had a son like me. I don't know.

When my pilot flew *my* ship, he always treated it as though he were on his way to church with his family. Easy does it, use only the power needed, use almost all of the available runway, climb slowly, gently… Start descending miles away from the landing site, touch down with a delicate flair. What a classy guy!

His inspections of the aircraft as a preflight or after scheduled maintenance by my crew and me were most thorough. He wouldn't fly if he found even the slightest problem. No "We'll catch it next flight" kind of thing for him. He expected us to be always on our toes and we were. Almost always.

Once my assistant left a cotter key out of the tail wheel assembly, resulting in the airplane "wobbling" a bit on taxiing. The boss didn't detect it, but one of us noticed it first. We corrected that one in a hurry. Then there was the time when I was beside the captain on a post maintenance test flight at about 6,000 feet above Galena when suddenly there was a blast of air that hit us from the back, causing the plane to buffet and shake as we came out of a shallow dive. We were only about 150 miles from the Soviet border in Galena and with the cold war on we were ever on the alert for the possibility that we might get too close and offend the Russians.

The first thing we thought of as that blast hit us was that we had been hit by a missile from a Soviet jet. My amazing pilot worked to get control and he actually told me that we might have to parachute down. I got ready to get out, hoping that I wouldn't get clobbered by any of the tail section on the way down. As he slowed our airspeed from about 140 knots down to 100, the buffeting eased, then stopped. In a surprisingly calm, but characteristic manner, he said, "It's okay, I've got it, at ease, soldier," to the most terrified kid west of the Pecos - *me!*

"Mayday, Mayday," we radioed to the emergency crew on the deck. But our landing was perfectly routine. We were followed to the maintenance area by several trucks. When we got out and looked at the airframe we couldn't find anything wrong! Then suddenly my assistant's big head popped out of the top of ole' Lucky Thirteen where a small window was missing from above the pilot's seat.

We doped it out later. When we were pulling out of that dive, the vacuum over the top of the plane pulled out one of the twin observation windows just above the pilot's head. That, in turn, created a vacuum in the passenger compartment that suddenly drew air from the rear, blasting open a rear baggage compartment, hitting us from the back and causing the rear of the craft to buffet wildly. There was no Soviet threat, no missile, no airframe damage and I, being my calm, self-assured self, had dealt with the situation in a most mature and routine manner.

An occasional happy day, or at least one that starts happy, will break the gloom-cycle for awhile, and one of them I remember occurred on May 9, 1954. Several good things happened that day. I turned twenty-one on that day. Also some new orders came through, one of which assigned me to hazardous duty pay and, therefore, I would get $50 more a month for risking a life that was worth about that much. Another was a report of my promotion to the rank of corporal. Altogether, I would find my paycheck bringing me about $175 more each month. Now, *that's* a happy day!

Got to celebrate, right? Well, celebrate I did. I damned near killed myself with alcohol! At the urgings of my peers, I started drinking beer early in the evening. Not being accustomed to the arts, I started to get wobbly about an hour later. Then, when I should have quit, I let those who were to blame (because I never am) talk me into having a few more beers, then a few more.

When I staggered out of the hall, I kept falling and was picked up by trusty buddies. Then we passed the aircraft control tower. For some reason unbeknown to myself (I found this out the next day), I began throwing full cans of beer at the tower. Fortunately, it was too tall for my range and two narrow for my aim. In the process, however, I fell hard on a remaining can of beer that was in my field jacket severely bruising a rib. Eventually I was thrown into a jeep and pitched out onto the dirt in front of our Quonset hut, where, crawling inside, I slept off one of the worst experiences of my life. Not recommended.

In the morning, when my pilot went down to the flight line, he found his airplane still cold and unfueled. His dedicated crew-chief was nowhere in sight. He tracked me down. Finding me moaning and heaving on my cot, he took pity on a miserable subordinate. His only comment was "Huard, if there had been a good woman, you'd be dead this morning."

That was one time he really could have reamed my tail if he had felt so inclined, but he didn't. Then there was another time, and it was one that had extremely serious implications. In fact, I will feel my anxiety level increase now as I write about what happened one day when I let my guard down and almost caused five people to lose their lives. Had the Lord not been with me that day, I could be carrying the guilt for those deaths. I could have been court martialed and been convicted of negligent homicide and sent for decades to a military prison.

Let me set the stage for what happened. Occasionally, the big brass would come to Galena to view the troops. That meant that my busy Beaver had to be scrubbed and prepped for their flights out to the tent camps where the surveying was being done. There were seven or eight camps on various hilltops, and bars and plateau clearings. The top Whig and his assistant officers included a full bird colonel, a major, a captain and a no-named lieutenant.

The colonel was just one step down from the rank of brigadier general. So, as you can image, this was a day when we all trembled a bit, like the day when the priest was coming to visit our class of fourth graders at St. Al's after a week of "fear conditioning" by the sisters. We had prepared for a week for the arrival of these executive officers from Elmendorf A.F.B., the base near Anchorage.

I saw to it that my work-horse of an airplane was spotless that day. I filled the tanks, checked the oil over and over again, aired the tires to within a tenth of a tenth of a pound of recommended pressure, etc. All seats were in place, all parachutes were arranged with the sparkling latches perfectly placed. The polished seatbelt buckles were positioned with disgusting military precision, shoulder harnesses ready to be latched around the precious monarch and his aides.

When they arrived, I stood at attention until my captain told me to help board the brass. After awhile, everyone in place, I saluted at attention as my pilot taxied to the runway. Soon, using the full length of the runway, the captain gently raised the Beaver's nose, and I watched as the plane got smaller and smaller as they headed for Kaltag. I listened as the full power was on for takeoff and thrilled at the smooth whine of that incredible engine. You would have thought that I was listening to Mozart, as did Soleieri, enraptured by the splendor of the eloquent sound.

No more than a half-hour later, I heard something very strange off in the distance. It was a sound both familiar and different at the same time. It was the whine of my Beaver, but punctuated with big explosions about every five to seven seconds or so. "Whirrrrr, BANG, whirrr, BANG, whirrrrrrrrrrrr, BANG, whirrrr, BANG!" Something was seriously wrong. I watched and listened nervously. Then I began to pray that they would make it to the end of the runway. I was terrified that they might crash into the pines or into the rows of gas drums nearby.

Soon, with the engine backfiring and struggling, they taxied up to where I was waiting and the pilot shut the engine down. I watched as the badly shaken officers climbed out and retreated into the nearby hanger. Each must have communicated with his maker that day.

I climbed under the plane and checked the gas drainage sump valve to see if, by some terrible error, there could be water in the gasoline. I was absolutely stunned when water poured out of that valve! Lots of water! I knew immediately that I was in real trouble. I mean big trouble, *really* big trouble.

In order to make this meaningful, I should explain how light aircraft were normally fueled in the field in those days. We had to pump 100 octane gasoline from fifty-five gallon drums by using a hand operated pump. It was very hard work. It takes a long time to fill an eighty gallon tank. The gas was pumped into the bowl of a big funnel that had to be covered with an equally large chamois (like the one you would use to dry off your car) which absorbs any water that might be going into the tank. We always "shammied" the gas, usually finding that our supply drum had little water.

That day was different. Apparently I had pumped gas from that one in a hundred drums that had water. Previously, I had pumped hundreds of drums and never got water anything like what I got that day. And, against a routinely used practice, I guess I didn't use a shammy. I still cannot believe it! Of all days to screw up...

Soon, several officers were out near the plane asking me what was wrong. Being the young, naïve, stupid, honest kid that I was, I confessed that there was water in the gasoline. I could have loosened a wire on a magneto, or on the electric powered fuel pump. I could have pinched a fuel line. I could have found a scuffed rotor. I could have "tricked" a number of things, but not me, not young, dumb, honest Corporal Huard. All my life I had been taught to confess... Like my totally honest hardware store dad, I humbly opted for the truth.

One of the officers, a major, exploded into a rage. He began to curse me, ordered me into the hanger, stood me up against the wall at attention and verbally thrashed me with his snarling face inches away from mine. It went on and on. I don't know how long it took, but I know it was a long time. I stood at attention, dying inside and trying not to show it, crying, but trying to be an army corporal and not letting him see me cry. That major broke me that day. Frail as I was when I was drafted into the army, basic training couldn't break me. Five days of sea sickness couldn't break me. But that major did. Maybe it was because as he was yelling at me I could still feel my dad's finger stabbing into my chest from years ago when I was in the wrong place at the wrong time shooting a BB gun in Texarkana, Texas. Silly, huh?

Strangely, my pilot never said a word to me about that incident. I can't express how much I appreciated his silence. He had good reason to take me apart, but he didn't. He must have known how I was hurting. He will always be gentle on my mind. For some very special reasons, I held greater respect for that captain than for any other man I ever met in my brief life up to that time, except for dad, of course, my dear, too-honest dad. "Why did you have to teach me to be so honest, Pop?"

For the next few months I tried to put some meaning into that experience. I thanked God over and over that no one had died because of my carelessness. I traced my every step that morning over and over again in my consciousness. I knew that I had shammied that gas. I always did. How could there have been as much as a gallon of water in that sump? What were the odds of my getting my first bad barrel on that specific day? I've never been able to answer those questions.

Did someone else intentionally try to down my aircraft when it was to be loaded with all of those high level officers? Did someone pour a gallon of water into that tank the night before? I know I shammied that gas. I would swear on the Bible that I shammied that gas. I will never know. What a tragedy that would have been!

What would have happened if my highly-skilled pilot had not been able to safely land Corporal Donald Huard's sputtering DeHaviland Beaver on that fateful morning? What would have happened if the aircraft filled with army officers crashed into the pines before reaching the runway? Over the last 60 years I have repeatedly asked myself that question. Would all aboard have been killed? Would six families have suffered the loss of their fathers or brothers as a result of Don Huard's failure to keep water out of the airplane's gasoline?

Surely, an investigation would have been conducted following such a tragedy. Is it likely that twenty year-old draftee Corporal Huard would have faced possible court martial to be tried for manslaughter or negligent homicide? If convicted, would I have ended up in a military stockade or federal prison? For how many years?

A staff sergeant fellow in our maintenance crew was always angrily expressing his hatred for officers. I suspected that he might have intentionally tried to sabotage my airplane during the night before, but I was afraid to accuse him of complicity. I had no proof. So, I said nothing.

However, I knew that I *had* shammied the gasoline that went into the fuel tanks. I *always* did. I can still hear the backfiring of that big radial engine as I prayed that they would make it onto the runway. Thank God! They made it! Thank God that what could have happened - didn't...

With my confidence slowing recovering over the next months, I continued to do my job - very carefully. I built a barrel rack and "engineered" a way that my pilot could "bomb" the tent camps with two half-filled drums of gasoline to be used in the 'copters. A jet canopy release worked as a bomb release, the barrels being dropped in rivers and lakes near the camps so that they wouldn't burst when they hit. My pilot learned to drop those drums in the water and actually bounce them up on the shore. This eliminated the need to make dangerous landings with drums of gas on board.

As the long days grew shorter near summer's end we prepared for the flight home. Somebody wanted to know if anyone knew anything about picture-taking. I volunteered and found myself as the official flight photographer with a brand new 16 mm movie camera and all of the film I could eat. I shot roll after roll, making a documentary film of our trip. *That* was great fun. Somewhere in the archives of the aviation detachment of the 30th Engineer's Base Topographical Battalion of the U.S. Army there's a technicolor film of that trip that was taken, but never seen, by Corporal Donald V. Huard. Damn, that's neat!

We traveled down to McGrath, then through that treacherous pass next to Mt. McKinley again, to Anchorage. Then, down through the Yukon Territory, I sat side by side with my special pilot as we flew through the entire western portion of the country of Canada. There we were in late September, looking off in the distance for our first glimpse of the approaching treasure, the Golden Gate Bridge.

Soon it was there. For the last time, I reached for the microphone and talked to Captain Paul over the intercom. "Thanks for getting me home safe, Captain," I said. Do you know what he said to me? "Thanks for keeping it flying, corporal. You did a good job." This, in spite of the fact that I had nearly cost him his life. Or, *had* I? I'll never know. His wife and kids were waiting for him when we touched down. A man showed up in a jeep to get the camera and the many rolls of film I had shot. I never saw Captain Paul again.

Fifty-two days later, I was on the road to Los Angeles to hug Shirley and pick up my car. It was dark when I got to my sister's apartment. She was just walking up the street after getting off of the bus from work. Seeing her, I yelled, "Hi, Red," and she snubbed me, thinking that I was just another fellow flirting with a pretty girl. "Hi, it's Don," I said. And then, I got my hug. I've often wondered if she remembers that day when I was, once again, a free man.

The L-20 "Beaver" - My Love
Galena, Alaska - 1953

When I *did* shammy the gasoline…

Fellow crew-chief David with our "sister-ship" at Galena. Assigned in pairs, our Beavers were real work horses landing in dirt clearings and on sandbars near the Yukon River. 1954

Where you don't want engine trouble…

Chapter Seven

From Drags to Riches

Getting out of the service for me was like getting out of prison. I never did understand how anyone could find a home in the army. I learned a month or so later by letter that a few of my buddies were a bit miffed because when I got my release papers I didn't even bother to say goodbye to anyone. I just threw my duffle bag on a bus and got the hell out. I suppose that was a bit inconsiderate, but I just wanted the whole episode to be over.

Years later I asked myself if the army experience had been a good one for me. Considering the terrible emotional shape that I was in when Uncle Sam called me and the stronger personality I became as a result of having to take a little rough necking, I would have to say that military life did have a positive influence on me.

Probably the major positive influence is the knowledge that I met my responsibility to my family and my country. I would hate to have to live out my life with the feeling that I had run from doing the things expected of me. While I'm glad none of my own sons or my daughter had to go into the military (I do not generally support the draft), I would like to think if any one of them were called, he or she would follow in dad's footsteps. One thing is for sure, being forcibly taken away from home sure makes home look great.

It's a little strange to think back about the day I returned home as a veteran. I slipped into the house and hugged mom as though I had simply been off for a day at school. Nine year-old younger brother

Kenny was on the floor in front of the TV set and I sneaked up behind him and tapped him on the shoulder. When he saw who it was, he started to cry. I don't know why I remember that, but I felt that he really had missed me and that his tears were his childish way of showing it. I've always felt close to Ken who is now over seventy. I sincerely hope that I have been as good a big brother for him over the years as Ray and Richard have been for me.

To my delight, my former boss at the Maytag store, offered to rehire me at my old job. It wasn't so long before I was making washing machine repair service calls again all over Phoenix. Then when things got slow there, I worked at another Maytag business, a larger outfit that sold and serviced a variety of the major brands of appliances.

I still dated Kathy for awhile after my service days. She was a student at Phoenix College at the time and seemed to be doing quite well. Eventually, she convinced me to try a semester at the school, but I wasn't sure I could handle it. My high school performance had been substandard by any measure. I was in no way prepared to take advantage of any academic skills I had acquired because I just didn't have any. Remember, all the way through high school I was interested only in girls and cars, not at all in getting an education.

I had matured a bit in the service, however, and when I had worked on a few hundred washing machines I began to ask myself if I really wanted to work on them for the rest of my life. That idea didn't appeal to me. Meanwhile, to my surprise, I found most of my classes quite interesting. Some of my teachers were especially fascinating, like Mr. Paul Merrill, who taught psychology in H-204, the same room where I would eventually teach the same subject for thirty-five years! Of course, I had no way of knowing that one day I would become, of all things, a college professor who would live his teaching career at Phoenix Community College.

The exams were very difficult for me. My lack of language skills, the result of complete boredom in my English classes at North Phoenix High, really hurt me at test time. I was not accustomed to expressing myself in written form. I had no real study skills. In high school I had spent my study time racing my cars up and down Central Avenue, flirting with girls I was fascinated by and afraid of. In high school I spent my time in English class trading amorous glances with Sharon, a much better subject for my attention than whatever Mr. Koerner had in mind.

At the end of the first full semester at Phoenix College I got a row of C grades. I dropped out of Introduction to Engineering because I couldn't figure out how to work a slide rule. My math skills were nonexistent. Lord knows how I even got those C grades in English 101, General Psychology, Biology, Introduction to Business and Bow and Arrow 101. Kathy's grades were all As and Bs.

I earned another row of Cs the next semester. Those were in English 102, Sociology, Developmental Psychology, Algebra, Typing and Run Around the Track. I was good at running around the track. After army life, which involved lots of running with an M-1 rifle held at port, I could run as long as the good athletes. I could show good times on the track. However, I didn't show up *on* time *to* the track much of the time. That's because I had to escort Kathy to her classes before I went to mine. Those things are important, you know. It's no wonder my grades were only Cs.

During the following term, Kathy chose to go to a different college and I continued at Phoenix College. While we continued to date for awhile, we each began to see problems with our relationship that resulted in a mutual agreement to date others. Then, after a little more time, we stopped going out altogether. I centered more on psychology classes with additional ones in history, economics and a variety of other areas, even a class in music appreciation and another in piano keyboard training. My music career was quite short-lived. I discovered that my odds against hitting any correct key on any specific occasion on the keyboard ran eighty-seven to one against, odds too high to handle.

I attended the University during the summer of 1956, taking Philosophy and Personnel Problems in Industry. I got a C and a D. Back at P.C., the next semester my grades improved slightly and my interest in psychology extended into the clinical areas, psychoanalysis, existential psychology and holistic psychology. I got my first B in Economics and an A in Business Law. In the spring of 1957 I earned the first of four college degrees, the Associate in Arts Degree at Phoenix College.

Beginning full-time study at the University was not easy. My grades for the first two years of my college work were not high enough for automatic acceptance. I transferred a mere 2.03 cumulative grade point index from the community college. It necessitated my entrance on a probationary basis. However, I had a degree and I was determined to get another, the Bachelor of Science Degree, which I acquired in the summer of 1958. The next summer (1959) I had completed all requirements for the Master of Arts Degree. Twelve years later, married and the father of four children by that time, I completed all requirements for the Doctor of Philosophy Degree in psychology with graduate level minors in business and criminology. That special year was 1971.

During the late 50s dad and mom sold the family home on Meadowbrook and bought a nice new three bedroom two bath home in Scottsdale, nearer to where dad worked at Motorola. Dad's health improved considerably, to the point that he was able to handle his draftsman responsibilities quite well. The new home was especially nice, spacious as compared to the old one. Mary was married and living in California by then and Kenny, the last of the Huard children was in high school. Mom and dad rented me a room at very low cost as I continued my education at the University.

During those years mom had lots of health problems complicated by severe depression that characterized much of her life. She was never a happy person. Hers was a natural tendency to see the negative side of things and to dwell on responsibility and hardship almost to the extreme. She never did cultivate any hobbies or interests other than those of the family. Sad as it sounds, I can honestly say that I never heard my mother sing. Overwhelmed by depression and chronic fatigue, she often required hospitalization.

Perhaps much of the problem with mom was the fact that she was an older daughter in a relatively poor family with eleven surviving children of thirteen mothered by Elmira Lucier, a French speaking woman from eastern Canada. In her teens, mom carried too much responsibility for the younger children. Then, as a married woman and mother herself she had three children in three years, and three to follow, the last being born when she was was in her forties.

Obsessively catholic, neither Elmira nor her daughter would have ever considered practicing birth control. In mother's case, her mental depression was complicated by the added dependence she developed on prescription medication. There were times when her dependence on tranquilizers ran out of control. Through her adult years, mom was unreservedly dedicated to the welfare of her kids, but she tended to assume the role of one given too much to handle, one treated unfairly by circumstance. For us, a happy smile from Viola was a rare treat, indeed.

It was during one of her depressed times that Ken and I decided to try to cheer her up by getting all members of the family to join together, to get mom and dad a special gift signifying our appreciation for their love. Because their old TV set was small and worn, we decided to get a new color television set for their living room. We selected a lovely Mediterranean style console and, while dad was at work and mom was at a neighbor's, we installed it and anticipated their return. I made a special audio tape to go with the set telling them of our love for them. Unfortunately, when mother returned home she didn't even notice the brilliant colors on the screen. She was so depressed and medicated at the time that all she wanted to do was sleep. When we finally called her attention to the set she became very embarrassed. Dad came home about that time and was immediately enthralled by what he saw. He was thrilled by the colors, the thought and the taped message. They enjoyed that set for many years.

Mom, of course, was not always like that. There were lots of better times, but she never seemed to be truly happy. This neuroticism was a way of life for her, one that did affect her children in an adverse way. I've often wondered why she could not have seen more of the positive side of life. She learned well how to pray, but never how to play. Perhaps too much piety, too many kids too quickly and too serious a mental tone prevented her from seeing the good fortune of a loving husband and healthy kids who survived the wars. Fortunately, the last of her eighty-seven years were more positive, but I often wish it could have been different for her during her forties and fifties, especially.

The closeness of the Scottsdale home to the University was most fortunate for young Don during the late 50s. Low rent, a loving mom and dad and super meals kept me close at hand. Even several years into my college education my interest in drag racing at the nearby Beeline Dragway persisted.

I bought a worn out 1937 Chevy Coupe, removed the little engine and installed a 1950 Olds Eighty-Eight V-8 engine 18" back of where any engine should be. Then I installed a 1930's LaSalle transmission behind that big engine and re-geared the rear end to a 411 ratio, making that car hot enough to win four trophies dragging in the C altered coupe class. I towed my dragster to and from the track with my "street" Olds sedan. My wreck of a race car got many a laugh at the track with its name printed on the side, "Coupe De Grace" (the final blow). Friends called it the "Coupe Disgrace."

I blame my brother Richard for getting me interested in drag racing. When I was just sixteen years old Richard and a few of his Detroit friends came to Phoenix in their customed cars on their way to the Santa Anna National Drag Races in Southern California. After visiting with mom and dad for a day or two and filling up on mom's macaroni and tomato soup that Richard had bragged about often to his friends all the way from Dearborn, Richard talked mom into letting me go with them to see the king of all drag strip races in existence at that time.

I had never been that far from home before. I had never dreamed I might get to see the race cars plastered all over the pages of Hot Rod Magazine, the book about what was important in life. What a memorable, exciting time I had! Richard raced his expertly chopped and channeled Pontiac Sedan, clocking in the eighties in the quarter mile. After a few runs my big brother asked me if I would like to take it for a run! "Why don't you just dust off Frank in that fancy green deuce coupe, he asked," teasing his buddy by implying that the Pontiac was faster.

When I put the Pontiac up next to Frank's coupe at the starting line I was so excited it was almost unbearable. When the flag went down I stomped the car into action. Frank and I left the line precisely together, were exactly side by side for the first 1/8 of a mile and went through the 1/4 mile trap in a perfect dead-heat! Richard cheered and claimed his car had won. Frank said he beat us by a foot or two. The officials called it even.

Now, I had made a mistake that actually cost us that race. Richard's Pontiac had an automatic transmission. I was so nervous during that run that when the transmission was supposed to go into second gear I lifted my foot off of the accelerator just enough to make it shift into third rather than second. I lost the second gear acceleration just long enough to lose my edge and the result was that Frank was able to stay right with me. If I hadn't missed that shift, we would have won by a car length! It didn't matter. I experienced the thrill of my young lifetime. When Richard found out, he teased Frank some more. "We beat the ole 'Deuce using only two gears," he said. No young fellow appreciated his big brother more than I did mine that day. *That* was livin'. *That* was a good day.

One day near the beginning of my senior year in college I stood in the back yard at home and admitted to myself that I just couldn't afford to keep my disgraceful coupe anymore. I needed $175 for my tuition at the University and didn't have it. I knew that it wasn't fair to keep asking mom and dad for help. Even though it about killed me, I put an ad in the paper for the car knowing that it was for an end to my drag racing career.

To my dismay, a fellow showed up, looked my gem over, listened to it run and offered me $160 for it. What could I do? I took the deal. I guess I would have handled it okay except for what that guy said to me after he handed me the cash. "I don't want that junk to drag, I just want the engine for my pickup." I was really pissed when he left. That was *not* a good day.

I was in my mid-twenties by then and getting a lot more serious about my schooling. The higher you go in the educational system, the tougher the classes become. More and more time must be spent in study. It is a process that is broadening for the degree candidate, but also serves to isolate him from other things. My life changed. My high school friends, my drag racing buddies and my earlier girlfriends all slipped into the past as I became more involved with the professors, laboratories and students at the University.

A very fortunate thing happened the very day I first arrived for counseling at the University. I stood in line for my turn to be interviewed by an elderly man who happened to be the chairman of the Psychology Department. I was loaded with questions to ask. "What classes should I take? How much will they cost? What days will they meet?"

He was a very soft-spoken person, a kind, gentle man who, two years later, would play a role in my development as a teacher. I didn't know it when I was being advised, but the very day of his death was to be the day I first began lecturing at the University.

While I was being advised by this senior professor, the phone on his desk rang and he talked to a new incoming teacher about a new lab that was being set up. It didn't involve me, so I tried to ignore what he was saying. When the conversation was over, he suddenly turned to me and asked, "Young man, are you looking for work?" When I told him that I was going to need at least half-time employment, he told the others in line to wait. "We'll be back in a minute," he said, grabbing me by the arm and walking toward the other end of the Old Lyceum building.

There was a big stage there, used for plays and stage productions over the years. "Could you help us build a lab up here," he asked? Well, I could, and I did. For the next two years I was a research assistant to a new professor, a laboratory oriented psychologist who taught me about the field of experimental psychology. When I got my master's degree in 1959, it was a degree in Experimental Methodology in the Behavioral Sciences.

I've often thought about how fortunate it was for me that the phone call by the researcher came at the precise moment that I was the student being advised by the chairman. Talk about luck! It could have been any other fellow besides me who got the break, but I was the one sitting at the right place at the right time. Are some things just meant to be?

The animal research done in the lab was concerned with the investigation of the effects of narcotic and tranquilizing drugs on learning tasks for organisms under environmental stress. The project was funded by a private company, Wallace Laboratories, through the National

Institutes of Health, a government agency. My job at first involved only care and treatment of the white rats used in the experiments, but evolved into areas of data collection and evaluation and eventually into report writing, some of which resulted in publications in the Journal of Comparative Psychology with my name as co-author.

I was proud of my work in that area as it seemed a considerable step up from wrench-jockey on the drag strip to research assistant in a University bioscience laboratory. One day I gave dad a tour of the lab. That was special for me and probably for him.

Meanwhile, I continued my class work and began to get a little encouragement by way of some more respectable grades. At last, I was learning how to study in depth, how to extract significant information and incorporate it into useful notes and how to efficiently collect notes in the classroom. I learned to listen to my professors in a more careful way. I recognized the fact that I could not sit in class day after day letting my brain wander off to my romantic interludes and hoped-for weekend dates. If I were to succeed, I would have to perform. I had to make myself sharp for those increasingly difficult exams.

Speaking of romance, I was dating some during my mid-twenties, but not much. Still extremely shy, I shunned any thought of becoming a fraternity fellow. The role just didn't fit. I was not the suave, macho, nice car, sharp dressing playboy type. Any girl that I dated quickly found out that I was no prize. I couldn't even toss a football through the hoop.

Wuanita thought I was kind of nice. She was a sweet, pretty girl who resembled Gale Storm, the girl who played the lead in one of the first situation comedies, *My Little Margie*, that ran on TV in the 50s. She lived in a dorm, but went home each weekend to Tolleson, way over on the far other side of Phoenix. I didn't mind driving my old thirty-six horsepower 1954 Renault car about forty miles to pick her up for Saturday evening dates, but she was a little above my class and our nonromance didn't last. She was very bright and sincere, probably is a great mom with four grown kids and a bunch of grandkids today.

Then, there was Noreen. Talk about a nonromance! A tall, lanky blonde who just loved partying. That was a real mismatch if there ever was one. She and her roommate Evelyn liked to call the airbase near

Phoenix and invite a few flyboys over for parties. We didn't last very long. I was far too serious, too studious, too academic for her. She was too active for me. I was one of a number of men she was dating and I finally told her that I was tired of standing in line for her time and attention. She wasn't amused by that. So much for tall, lanky blondes. They *do* have more fun. Clearly not the Renault type...

Sometime in 1958, Jimmy Klink (the longtime friend who accompanied Shirley and me on that slippery clutch trip to Los Angeles) and I decided to attend a dance at the local Catholic Church on Central Avenue. On Saturday evenings the social group called the T G A (To Get Acquainted) held their biweekly dances for the young lonelies and we decided to attend. Then, we called it "looking for somebody nice." Now, young people call it "cruizin' for chicks."

Marie was one of the girls I got courage enough to ask for a dance that evening. I did my best, which was probably not very well. She danced well, was very friendly and surprised me by telling me that she had come to town from Minnesota several years earlier as one severely handicapped by arthritis. As with dad, the Arizona sun and low humidity had given her a new lease on life.

How can I describe now, fifty years later, the young fourth-grade teacher I met that evening who would be my marriage partner for twenty-three years and the mother of our four beautiful children? Today, my children ask me to tell them what their mother was like, how we met, fell in love and decided to marry. They lost their mother when she was just forty-nine and they would like me to restore my memory of her. I will try.

Marie and I were both twenty-six when we met. I was a University student working on my Master's degree, she was a teacher trained at a small college in Minnesota. I can remember what she was wearing the evening I first met her. It was a soft olive-colored short sleeved shirtwaist dress, with a matching belt. She told me weeks later that she and her friend Mary Clark had been out shopping earlier in the day and hadn't even planned to attend the dance that night. Some of their other friends were going, however, so the girls decided to drop by. I'm so glad they did.

I saw her at several of the following dances and eventually got the nerve to ask if I could call her "sometime," which was about as quick as I could find a telephone. Typical of the usual graduate student at that time, I was so broke that I couldn't afford expensive entertainment for my dates. How wonderful it was that it didn't matter to her!

We began our dating with trips to the Phoenix Public Library, where she graded papers for her fourth-grade students and I poured over my notes in preparation for my exams. We often laughed at each other because we had to break our hand holding to turn the pages of what we were each reading. She always wore dresses, always looked so prim and proper with her hair drawn back into a teacher's pony tail.

On the weekends we went to Encanto Park. We walked hand in hand, stood close together on the bridge over the murky lagoon, tossing peanuts or whatever to the local wildlife. Once I climbed up onto the stage of the band shell and sang loudly (and badly) to her until she pleaded with me to stop.

When we could get enough money together, we would go to play goofy-golf. If we were really in good shape, we could stop for a hamburger at the Polar Bar Drive-in. Occasionally we went to a movie. One time at goofy-golf, Marie, dressed in a beautiful red sweater and a long grey flannel skirt, managed to accidentally hit the ball into the cup on the first stroke. She knelt on the carpet for just a moment to reach into the cup for the ball. As she did, she tossed her head back, gleaming and laughing, then looked up at me with a brilliant smile on her face and absolutely took me apart! That was it. I was a goner from that time forward.

Because Marie was so catholic, we always went to mass together on Sunday morning. After church one day, I brought her home to meet mom and dad. We spent only a half-hour or so with them, but it was nice. Another shirtwaist dress, yellow with springtime flowers for Easter, spotlessly clean and perfectly pressed. When I came home later in the day, dad said, "Son, don't let that one get away." I'm so glad I didn't.

She was about 5'2" tall with soft blue eyes and that smile. It wasn't that she was always smiling. She, too, was a serious, pious, hardworking girl. It was fun to watch her conducting a class of those fourth graders who obviously adored Miss Fournier, the lady who now had a crew-cut boyfriend. Her fellow often picked her up after school. The little girls would giggle when they saw me waiting for her outside the door. The bolder ones would tease their teacher. "Miss Fournier's gotta boyfriend. Neah, Neah."

After Marie and I became engaged to be married, the nuns at the convent at St. Thomas School invited us over for a lovely dinner. I was quite uncomfortable in the presence of so much holiness. I felt like I was at my last supper, being at the table with all of those hooded ladies who were so dedicated and pure and being in surroundings that were cleaner than anything I had ever scrubbed while I was in the army. It was obvious that the sisters had made that evening very special to us all. Never had I met so many people with such sweet intentions. They were truly lovely people, none nicer than the one who happened to be Marie's sister, Sister Joyce Fournier, who was also teaching at the school.

At that time, when you were planning to marry a catholic girl, notably one who was sheltered by a host of nuns at the school where she worked as a lay-teacher, you had to attend meetings with the pastor of the church to be prepared for catholic marriage. You can imagine how much I enjoyed several sessions with Father John Doran, Marie's pastor, boss, and personal counsel on matters of the purpose of marriage and the evils of birth control. Oh, boy!

We were promptly supplied with a big book called The Catholic Marriage Manual which was a treatise on what we should and could do, but more importantly what we couldn't do, namely, have a fun time. Father Doran was great. I thought he was a terrific human being. Marie and all of the sisters respected him as an exceptionally understanding and honorable priest. He conducted our marriage ceremony on June 13, 1959.

The marriage manual was clearly a catholic production dedicated to, more than anything else, the production of more catholics. The book was based on the assumption that there were specific rules of marriage to follow and that if you disagreed with any of them it was because you lacked sufficient education on those matters and required further enlightenment by the authors of the book. Of course, the Pope was on their side.

The rhythm method of birth control was favored as a promotional tool for increasing the sales of catholic calendars. It offered a method for the prevention of conception that was so effective that it nearly always resulted in pregnancy within one year. Marie and I never did catch on to the system so we had three children within three years. Then, when we really concentrated on it and got everything down smooth, we had twins! Four of the five children we had in the first six years of our marriage survived. If we had been any more obedient to Rome, we could have had even more.

Now, it's tempting to say that the rhythm method doesn't work. That's not true. It works quite well, for Catholicism… Not that we were sorry that we had so many kids. However, it would have been nice if we had been able to understand. Maybe we got it wrong. Maybe we weren't very bright. Maybe we were just too much in love. Maybe it had something to do with the music.

Marie was always interested in my strong motivation for higher education. She knew I wanted to be a doctor of psychology and willingly went through years of limited resources and the effects of my high stress levels just because she knew how important it was to me. She and our children went without a lot of nice things that others enjoyed because of *my* stubborn egocentric need to prove to the world that I could finish my Ph.D. program.

So there we were, with four kids, well into our thirties, "daddy" still determined to show his greatness by getting that Ph.D. degree. Was my drive toward the completion of my program a mark of dedication and courage or was it a selfish act, perpetrated at the expense of a loving wife and our children?

Looking back at it now, I know the answer. It *was* worth the effort.

Toast to Bride and Groom

Don and Marie were married
on June 13, 1959

In Memory

Marie Fournier Huard
in her late twenties

1932 - 1981

the kids, five, four
and six months

1966

Chris, Theresa, David and Gregory

Chapter Eight

"Congratulations, Don..."

Marie continued to teach at St. Thomas School after our summer wedding and I, having completed my master's thesis, was in possession of my first graduate level degree. I was working about thirty hours per week in the Psychology Department at the University. We rented a single bedroom apartment on 32nd Street, not far from Marie's school.

Midway through the school year, Marie began to disturb the clergy at the school by revealing that the rhythm method had worked and she was soon to become a mom. One day she was invited into the principal's office and advised that it was time for her to leave the school because when you were in a "family way" at that time, especially at a catholic school, you belonged home rather than with the young impressionable fourth-grade students.

She could have worked longer into her pregnancy and, indeed, did exactly that, taking a job as a receptionist for several family physicians. She worked very hard at that job, right up until two weeks before the birth of our first son, Christopher Leon Huard.

It was up to me to provide the income for our family in the years following and I did as best I could. Still, because I insisted on staying at the University and continuing with classwork as well as my part-time job, our yearly income for the first few years was only about $3500 plus what I could earn during the summers when I worked as a mail boy in the office of the Standard Oil Company in downtown Phoenix. My G I benefits of $135 monthly had run out by the time I finished my bachelor's degree, so it wasn't long before we began borrowing from the government on a program called the National Defense Education Act.

In desperation, I even petitioned my big brother Ray for help in the amount of $50 per month, which I'm sure was not very easy for him to send us from California where he had to maintain his own apartment. Living in Palo Alto has never been cheap.

I guess I presented him with a quite convincing plea when I told him about my interest in a teaching career as we had lunch at the Helsing's Restaurant in Scottsdale when he was visiting Phoenix. I remember that as we checked out of the restaurant, an elderly stranger who had overheard our conversation said to Ray, "If you can, you should help that young man." For a year and a half, Ray sent a check each month. Years later, I paid him back. Needless to say, I still appreciate his kindness.

My chairman saw me coming down the stairs of the old Lyceum Building one afternoon and told me something that threw me into an absolute panic. "Congratulations," he said to me. "Sir?" I responded, not having the foggiest what he was talking about. "Don, you have been selected by the faculty advisory committee to be the very first of our 'potential" doctoral candidates to present his master's thesis before the faculty-graduate student conference being held next month." "Oh Boy," I thought. "Thanks a bunch."

I had spoken to classes before as I gave seminar reports and was doing a little teaching of freshman students in Psychology 101, but had never faced the faculty as the guest speaker for a one-hour symposium. I had to escape from such a responsibility, to be sure. I mean, how in *hell* was I going to handle *that* one?

I thought of suicide. I thought I might call in sick on the day of the seminar. I thought I might plan a coronary for that day. I even thought of reenlisting in the military. After all, didn't they say I could be the crew-chief on a DeHaviland Otter, the big brother to the Beaver, if I would re-up for three more years? It was a sixteen seat plane with a 650 horsepower radial engine!

As the day for my appearance neared, I saw brochures on campus announcing my "program." I was to be entertainer of the month, whether I liked it or not. I didn't like it, but, by golly, I did it anyway.

I even brought my pretty wife Marie to the campus so that she could see what I planned to do. She sat in the back of the room in her very best $8 deep blue, flowered dress and suffered through it with me She looked so pretty in that dress.

The title of my master's thesis was *Desensitization: The Effects of Narcotic and Tranquilizing Medications on Organisms Under Stress*. How appropriate! However, that's just academic lingo for what drugs do to rats. About forty people attended my presentation, fifteen of them professors from the Department of Psychology and Philosophy. I really didn't want to be there. I missed my army airplane! I missed Galena! I missed olive drab. I even missed my First Sergeant!

There is a very complex data analysis technique used by those in academic research called the analysis of variance. After a researcher collects mountains of data, those data are evaluated mathematically by using different "cells" for data from the organisms treated under each of a variety of experimental conditions. The variability of the data *between* the treatment cells is compared to the variability of the data *within* the cells to determine if the treatment (drug) effect was greater than any extraneous or chance effect that might have occurred. The overall chance effect is shown by the variability of the data *within* the cells. By comparing between-group variance with within-group variance, the investigator can determine if the drug effects were significantly greater than any effects that might have occurred by chance or unknown factors.

I became determined in my preparation for that seminar that I was not going to limit my presentation to just the procedures and results of my experimentation. I decided to attempt to explain the analysis of variance technique to the attending graduate students as well. Although not a mathematician, I felt that I knew the logic, the calculation steps and the interpretation process well enough to convey them in that seminar.

At one point, as I went through the steps, I saw my professor mentor begin to shake his head from side to side. I changed a detail or two and he began to move his head up and down and grin with satisfaction. I knew I was getting it right.

I thanked everyone for attending as I finished and got a delightful surprise. Faculty members and students were applauding! Not politely, but enthusiastically! One professor, a clinical practitioner, shook my hand and said, "Don, you should be a teacher." My chairman commented positively on my speaking ability. Several other professors praised me to my sweet Marie, who probably understood little of the technicalities of the topic I had covered.

It was conveyed to me a day or two later that a social psychologist and behavioral research specialist had told one of the graduate students, "If that's the kind of candidate we will have in our new doctorate program, we won't have to worry about being a second rate school."

The best thing for me on the day of the seminar was the effect that the day's efforts had on Marie's understanding of what I did at the University. She was inclined from that day forward to better understand my intense desire to complete my doctorate program.

Just after our son Chris was born, Marie and I were able to beg, borrow and save up enough money to place the smallest possible down payment on our first home, a little bonded, brick, three-bedroom home in Scottsdale, Arizona. The brand new Hallcraft Home sold for $11,250. Our house payment was $188 per month. Soon, our daughter Theresa was born. She was our second child in just two years.

We were so proud of our kids, Chris with his reddish hair and fair skin and his little sister who was the prettiest child God ever created. We were so broke most of the time, but we were in love with each other, with our family and with the great good fortune of having our two beautiful kids.

The genuine quality of the lady I had married came through one day that serves sweetly in my memory. We were downtown shopping at the JCPenney's store about two months before Theresa was born. We pushed Chris' stroller onto the escalator to the basement bargain area (Chris in his mother's arms) to get some badly needed diapers. Marie fondled the cute little baby underpants and printed colorful rubber pants in the baby department. She loved the printed nightshirts especially. We couldn't buy any of them because we just didn't have the money.

As we came back up the stairs with one-dozen diapers and nothing else, I agonized over what to do about the fact that the next day was my wife's birthday and I was completely broke. At the top of the escalator, I said to her, "Honey, I don't have any money for a gift for your birthday, but I do have the credit card and I would like you to pick out something nice for yourself that you would like to have that costs $10 or so. Maybe a dress, a sweater, some favorite cologne, something special for you."

Marie spun the stroller around immediately and headed back down to the baby department. In spite of my urging her to get something for herself, she picked out three tiny nightshirts, another dozen diapers, and several plastic rattles for her babies. "That's all I want," she said with her eyes sparkling. Is it any wonder that I treasured her and treasure that fond memory?

In 1962, my advisor at the University reluctantly suggested that I had better leave the school for awhile and get a better paying job in view of my increasing debt and the critical needs of our family. I learned of a job opening in the personnel department at Motorola where dad worked. I applied for the job and was interviewed, but did not get hired. When I called several weeks later to see if I was still being considered, I was told that in my interview I had sounded too enthusiastic about an academic career. Apparently, they assumed that I would not stay at Motorola if they hired me. I also applied that year for a new full-time teaching position at Phoenix College, but was not even called in for an interview.

I continued with coursework toward my Ph.D. degree. I also assisted the elderly Dr. Skinner with the teaching of his Psychology 101 classes. I would sit in the back of the room and write test questions based on his lectures. They were incorporated into the students' exams. He lectured on Mondays and Wednesdays and I would conduct review sessions with the students on Fridays.

Imagine how I felt, looking at the cleared bulletin board in the department office one day at the tiny card that said, "Doctor H. Clay Skinner - Chairman of the Psychology Department, passed away over the weekend." I was asked to complete his classes for the semester, as if I could have replaced his sincere, competent skills when I was just at the beginning of the development of my own. I did my best. The following semester I was assigned classes of my own to teach as a part-time lecturer at the University. I was twenty-eight years old at the time.

Early in 1963, I applied again for a teaching position at Phoenix College. I was interviewed, but nothing happened. Hoping to be called back for another interview, I waited and waited and still there was no word. I knew that I had not represented myself well in the interview. In fact, as I left the dean's office, I was very angry at him, his interviewing methods and at myself for my own stupidity. Considering how badly we needed that job for me, I felt as though I had been a victim in a major disaster.

Upon reflection, I now know that the lesson that the dean taught me that day was invaluable. He made a significant contribution to the success of my professional academic career on that day. Today, I would shake his hand and thank him for a lesson well taught by a pro.

The interviewing dean began with routine pleasantries designed to relax the applicant. He asked me about my experience, about my continuing efforts to complete my doctoral studies, a little bit about my family, etc. Then, his demeanor began to change. His questioning took on a rather strange twist. "Don," he said, "we don't hire on the basis of a candidate's political ideology here at the college; however, I am interested in you as a person. I'm interest in your attitude about the kind of world our students are facing these days."

He continued, "Would you characterize yourself as rather liberal or conservative in your point of view? And why?" I remember answering with a leaning toward the conservative side, but I also remember quickly becoming annoyed that I would be asked such a question. Further, I became painfully aware in a very short time of how I was unsure of what those words meant.

What, precisely, is the difference between a liberal and a conservative? His next question was even more difficult to answer. "What do you think should be done about the serious problem developing in Laos," he asked? I had to answer in such a way that it must have indicated that I didn't know anything at all about the political conflict that had, by then, led us into the Vietnam War.

A few additional questions about social issues that were *outside* of the academic world left me reeling. I left the interview angry, frustrated and feeling wholly inadequate. I had presented myself as a qualified teacher of psychology, complete with a placement file and history set up at the University placement center. My photograph, my transcripts, my work experience and my letters of recommendation were all in proper order and placed before him. Then I bombed the interview! Dumb! Dumb! Dumb!

Over the next thirty-five years, I told the students in my many classes about that experience and what it taught me. After that interview I visited the world of deep depression for the next few months. I was so devastated that I actually made a subsequent appointment to see the dean again. Then, I presented a clearer case for my appointment as a faculty member at the college.

He must have thought that to be a rather brash move. The dean quietly listened to me and as I left, I felt that at least I had impressed him with my sincere desire to be of service to the students at Phoenix College. I felt a little better, but still, there was no word.

The lesson I learned was a painful one. It was that I had narrowed my field of study through all of my college career to only those things of my own specific interest. I took mountains of psychology classes. I assumed that education is acquired only on the college campus, so I never bothered with the reading of the local newspaper about what was happening in the world. I always watched situation comedies and sports programs on the television and never a newscast. When I drove to and from the University on a daily basis for a decade, I always turned my car radio to my favorite top forty music. I never listened to the news.

I had set myself up for what happened on the day of my humbling interview. The interviewer simply wanted to know if the person he was considering as an advisor to the students of the college was himself well advised about the problems of the times. Was this prospective professor up on current events, on happenings in the world? Clearly he was not. You had better believe, I took measures to correct that situation after being taught by the pro. Thank you, Doctor... You taught me a big lesson.

In my later academic training at the University, I took more varied classes. Classes in political science, economics and criminology and urban affairs. They helped to broaden my background. I became a solid A and B student by then, showing more discipline and determination than ever. I got beyond the used Chevy ads and the sports pages of the *Phoenix Gazette* and into the editorial pages. I listened to the daily news.

Continuing with my doctoral studies, I had trouble with the foreign language requirements. A year of French, then I failed the two-hour, sixty-line translation exam. That was a big disappointment. I studied more, then passed it on my second attempt. I got the graduate council to accept a second minor, in criminology, in lieu of the requirement for a second language. That involved twenty-one hours of graduate credit. I got all As and Bs.

Next came the final comprehensive examinations. Those exams are the handwritten finals covering your coursework. They are the toughest you take, other than the oral dissertation defense which is the one that, if successful, completes the Ph.D. program. The "comps" consisted of twelve hours of writing in a two-day period over four specific areas of psychology as predetermined by a graduate committee. Agreed upon were the following four areas: The History of Psychology, The Psychology of Learning, Research Design and Statistics and Behavioral Modification in Clinical Psychology.

I buried myself in my student cubicle in the department for a full year in preparation for those comprehensive exams. I passed every one of them. I wrote for six and a half hours on Sunday and six more hours the very next day which was Labor Day, of 1963. All that I needed to successfully finish my program was the completion of a doctoral dissertation and the defense of it before my graduate committee and I would be Dr. Huard. I was to find, years later, that that would be the toughest challenge.

Good things happen too. As the time for my comps came near I came home from school late one afternoon to find Marie holding a long envelope addressed to me from Phoenix College. "Wow," I thought, "a request that I come in for another interview." Nearly $10,000 in debt by then, I went into orbit when I discovered that the envelope contained a contract for full-time teaching in the Department of Psychology at the college! The dean had come through! My salary would be $6394, a significant increase over my earnings for previous years. The very next day after the Labor Day on which I wrote the last of my comps at the nearby University, I started my orientation and my teaching career at Phoenix Community College.

Chapter Nine

Lab Rats and Rug Rats

While at the University in 1962, I worked for Dr. Jack Michael, an especially effective teacher in the area of operant conditioning. He had developed a lab located on the third floor of the new Social Science Building in which students worked with white rats, using them to illustrate the basic principles of conditioning as contributed to the field of psychology by the world famous Harvard behavioral psychologist, B.F. Skinner.

Called *reinforcement theory* by some, the Skinnerian interpretation of animal and human behavior is that all learned behavior patterns are shaped by their consequences. Another way to say it is that when responses occur and are followed by some form of reinforcement (reward), they tend to be repeated and are strengthened. Reinforced behavior is increased in frequency.

Socialization on the human level is seen as behavior *shaped* by parents who, for instance, reinforce the use of appropriate words by a child as the language system develops. Parents strengthen obedient, socially responsible responses as the child is guided toward maturity. The child's personality, attitudes and behavior are seen as reflective, therefore, of the parents' ability to mold the child into a responsible adult by using appropriate reinforcing techniques.

In Dr. Michael's lab, freshman and sophomore psych students were assigned white rats to use as experimental subjects. They used the principle of reinforcement to shape lever pressing, chain pulling, nose touching responses on cue. In this way they showed how behavior can be molded and shaped and placed under the control of specific environmental stimuli by manipulating the available sources of reinforcement (in this case, small pellets of food).

It was a fun lab for the students. Lectures were given that explained principles of behavior such as extinction (the weakening of behavior), stimulus generalization, stimulus discrimination (as in control of behavior at a traffic light) and response chaining. It was a fun lab to teach, as well. Using Skinner Boxes and electronic control panels, I learned much about relay circuitry, this being long before the advent of the computer chip.

When I started working at Phoenix College I emphasized laboratory techniques in my Psy 101 classes, even though we had no lab. When I had a dean sitting in the back of the room doing his evaluation of my skills (?), somehow the topic for the day would be the laboratory assessment of behavior. I emphasized how students at the University were conditioning rats to illustrate conditioning principles and how those principles could be used to analyze the behavioral patterns of humans. When another dean showed up, I did it again. Of course, I hoped that a few "powers that be" would authorize a few bucks to enable Don Huard to set up the first psychology laboratory at Phoenix College. They did. And so, I did.

Marie and I decided in early 1964 that we needed a little bigger home for the raising of our family which was going to increase in size by one in November. We looked at the ones we could afford in Starlight Park, but fell in love with a bigger one in a west Phoenix development called Frontier Estates. It was a four-bedroom, two bath, ranch-style home in Maryvale.

We had not used my GI home Loan benefit for our first home purchase, so we applied for a veteran's loan to purchase this $14,500 dream house. We were turned down because of inadequate income. However, I wrote a long letter to the Veteran's Administration telling them what a war hero I had been and how we were managing our other house on much less income and they reconsidered and give us the loan!

Marie's third pregnancy was a troubled one. She was sick more of the time than had been the case with Chris and Theresa. She was anemic and lacked energy, but then, chasing the other two around the house all day would tire anyone. We watched and waited not only for the birth of number three, but also for the building of our new home through that long, hot Phoenix summer. When school started again in late August, we were about a month away from move in day, so we were very excited. It was a difficult time, but a good time.

During a quiet weekend, my wife confided in me that she was a bit concerned about the fact that the previously active baby she was carrying seemed to be unusually inactive. "He hasn't kicked all day," she said. "I wonder if something is wrong."

On Monday morning I dropped her off at the doctor's office and went to teach my first class. It was my intention to pick her up after my class, take her home and return to the campus to finish out the day. I wasn't in the class very long before a school messenger brought me a request to call the doctor's office immediately. "The baby has died," Marie cried into the phone. I dismissed my students and went immediately to the doctor's office.

The doctor couldn't give us an explanation as to why it happened. It wasn't a problem of poor diet or poor medical care. It wasn't anyone's fault. It just happened. The doctor began to question me about Marie's emotional stability, her tendency towards depression. Then he suggested something strange to us. "It would be better," he said, "if you could carry this pregnancy through to its natural conclusion."

This meant that Marie would not be induced into labor, but would continue instead, to carry the baby until its full term. It was a difficult decision for us all. Bless her heart, she waited, day after day, for three weeks before labor began and then she delivered a stillborn child.

During those days of waiting, I kept Marie occupied with thoughts of our new home as much as possible. Each day we went out to see the progress that had been made by the craftsmen. When we picked out our floor tile and carpeting, when we watched the roof being shingled, when we did our walk,-through, when we moved in, we still felt the sense of loss that was to be a reality when the baby was born. Afterward, while

Marie was still in the hospital, I carried the little lamb skin-covered casket to the gravesite at Saint Francis Cemetery. We named our lost little girl Mary Ann.

A year or so later, we were again expecting an addition to our young family. The baby was active and Marie seemed stronger. There was less morning sickness and her doctor kept advising us that all signs were positive. Yet, fear of a repeat of what happened a year earlier kept us on edge. We prayed for a healthy child, this one to be our last whether or not the Pope would agree.

During the fifth and sixth months, Marie began to look frail and drawn. Her blood count went down. She had swelling of her feet that was similar to that which occurred in the previous pregnancy. Dr. DioGuardi advised us that all was well. However, as the weeks went by, we became more concerned.

One evening well into the seventh month, Marie began to experience labor pains. First subtle, then not so subtle. The pains persisted. I called Dr. D. "You get her over to Saint Joe's as fast as you can!" he yelled into the phone. As we drove through the darkened Phoenix streets we held hands, each of us quietly avoiding any mention of the possibility that we were losing another child. Finally Marie said, "Dr. DioGuardi thinks this baby's dying too, doesn't he?" I said I didn't think it would happen again. I said it, but I wasn't convinced that we weren't going to be disappointed again.

When you enter the hospital, even if you are about to expire, you absolutely must be cleared by that lady whose job it is to see that the bill is paid. Usually, it's a lady in her forties who is totally indifferent to such things as moans and screams of pain and any sense of urgency other than the need to get your insurance number and your zip code.

Getting my frightened wife past that lady was a real chore. "How long have you been at this address," she asked. "How long has your husband worked at Phoenix College?" "Who the *hell* cares," I thought, but didn't have the nerve to ask. That lady belonged with the IRS, not as an admittance clerk in a hospital!

How I appreciated the words of the big daddy doctor who first examined Marie when we finally got past Lady Accountable! He came out to greet me in the hall and said "Don't be alarmed, sir, we know what you folks went through a year ago. This time, there's a strong heartbeat and everything is just fine." He was a huge fellow with tiny glasses way out on the end of his nose. His face was filled with understanding kindness.

I was sent down to the "pacing" room for prospective dads. I waited there as patiently as I could, watching TV without seeing it. I looked at magazines that had no stories for me. Suddenly, the door burst open and a short, roundish German-sounding lady with no back to her head, dressed in surgical green, was mispronouncing my name. She seemed very excited. "Meester Hooooored," she said, "Commonzee! Commonzee! Dahs babeeses isa inna inkaabaturs!"

I had no idea what she meant, but in view of the fact that I was the only "Meester" in the room, I smartly concluded she meant me. So, I followed her down the hall. Soon a wheeled incubator was before me with the tiniest baby I had ever seen. It was my new son David weighing in (or out) at 3 lbs., 4 oz.

I was absolutely delighted. Then, out of the corner of my eye I detected a second incubator approaching with a baby that made David look large by comparison. Gregory checked in at 2 lbs., 13 oz! Twins! We had twin sons! On the way to St. Joe's we prayed for a healthy baby and suddenly we had two! My wife, still in a fog because of the anesthesia, asked me, "Does *he* have all his parts?" "*He* sure does, honey," I said, "even a second set."

I just did not believe that those were *our* babies. I denied that it was possible. In my own psychology lectures, I had covered the topic of multiple birth many times, yet I never thought of it as a possibility for the Huards. Dr. D later told us that an x-ray revealed the two babies an hour or so before they were born (no such thing as routine ultrasound for expecting moms way back in 1965). He was there for the delivery and he was so happy for us. *That* was a terrific night!

I called dad at Motorola the next morning. "Hey dad," I crowed. "How's that for a rendezvous in space?" Would you believe that the birthday of the twins was December 15, 1965, the actual day of the first rendezvous in space between a Russian and an American astronaut? Check it out…

Babies born so tiny are not usually released from the hospital for weeks. It took three weeks for David to reach five pounds and be ready to go home. It took Greg about a month longer than that. Because they were both in incubators the costs were doubled and overwhelming. But then, I had hospitalization coverage for employees in the college district. Except for one small detail. In the policy there was a rarely noticed exclusion, "Children not covered until thirty days after birth."

You can spend lots of money in a hospital in thirty days. Added to my educational debt of $10,000, the $9,500 hospital bill sent me to my credit union for help. A lady I will never forget, Evelyn Firth, arranged a loan used to pay the hospital bill. I paid it back over the next four years, in not very easy installments.

Needless to say, I was a proud dad. Good marriage, good job, new home, beautiful kids and a new set of twin sons. Life is good. Even if it does mean that we were up nights, staring blank-eyed at each other as we fed our fascinating little "preemie" boys, even if there was little time for anything else besides changing diapers, fixing bottles, walking the floors and trying to survive.

It was really tough on Marie. It took several years for her to regain reasonably good health. Emotionally she held up well, but there were so few times that she could get away to enjoy being herself. We hardly ever had time together away from the kids. Just like mom and dad, we didn't take time to enjoy one another as we should have.

Knowing what I know today, I would have taken Marie out to a movie every two weeks even if I had to teach Saturdays to do it. Knowing what I know today, I would have fed her restaurant food at least once per week. With what I know today, I would have encouraged her to go out with friends occasionally while I babysat with the kids. Knowing what I know today, I would have recognized how little I knew then, about the kind of mom she was.

Marie's parents were good people. Mr. and Mrs. Leo J. Fournier raised five children in the small town of Warren, Minnesota. Dale, Joyce, Marie, Charles and Judy were raised as the children of the local baker and his wife Ann. They never owned a home like the Huards, instead they lived above the bakery and all of the kids worked there from time to time. Leo had only a grade school education. He was a very quiet man, concerned enough about Warren to let himself be elected mayor of the town. The kids called him a "big fish in a little pond."

He was sensitive about his lack of education and opened up to very few people. Fortunately, I did learn a great deal about him one evening as we took a very long walk after dinner at our home. I learned about how much it hurt him to lose his oldest son Dale when the young man was only in his early forties. I learned about how proud he was of his family, but how difficult it was for him to express his feelings. I learned about how much he missed Joyce, Marie and Judy when they went to Arizona, far from where they were raised. I learned about how he helped Chuck set up his own bakery in nearby Thief River Falls.

After retirement, the Fourniers sold the bakery and bought a double-wide mobile home in Warren and a Winnebago motor home that they used for traveling to Phoenix for several winters. They rented a space in a mobile home park in Scottsdale. Often they would come to see their grandkids or we would take our family to see them and play shuffleboard on the park court.

Sister Joyce left St. Thomas School in Phoenix sometime in the mid-70s, returning to the St. Scholastica Priory in Duluth, Minnesota to teach and care for the elderly in her religious order. Presently, she runs her own photography and picture framing studio and sends us beautiful samples of her work. Her life has always been characterized by service to others, either as a teacher or as an administrator of custodial care. God blesses her, I'm sure. I know that we do.

Judy, the youngest and orneriest of the Fournier kids, spent her own career as a Motorola employee in Tempe, Arizona. She has recently retired. Judy is a special part of our family. Aunt Judy, like Aunt Joyce, is close to the kids and remains an active part of their lives. It is a consideration that means a lot to them, as it does to us. She usually shows up for special family holidays, but often says she's glad they are our kids, not hers. As she reads this, I can hear her mumbling, "You've got that right, buddy."

Grandma Ann Fournier passed away in Scottsdale in the mid-70s. Grandpa Leo joined her a few years later. I remember them both very kindly, especially meeting them just one day before my wedding to Marie in 1959. After the ceremony, I asked them if it was all right for me to call them mom and dad. They seemed amused at my request, but I was always proud to do so. They were part of what made our lives good.

Twins are marvelous to watch. Twins are so close to each other that they tend to develop their own little language system. David often served as an interpreter between Greg and his parents, telling us what Greg "means" when he asked for something. David tended to take a little advantage, at times, as kids are apt to do. Greg was prone to howl in protest when frustrated by his brother. Each learned rather quickly the meaning of the words, "*He* did it!"

When the Huard family went shopping, mom and dad discovered that two infant seats would fit sideways, crosswise in a single shopping cart. We spent a lot of time talking to people who would stop to look at the twin boys. Anyone who had twins in their own family simply had to tell us about them. Once, a huge, plumber-type man loaded down the pipe fittings almost dropped them all when he saw David and Greg. Then, he said the sweetest thing. "Twice blessed," he said.

An elderly lady who reminded me much of Elmira Lucier, my own French-speaking grandmother, saw us in the grocery store. She was very old fashioned like granny, wearing a loose print dress, carrying a flowered carpet-type handbag and missing more than a few teeth. "Oooohh, Gawd luvumm," she wailed.

We joined a small exclusive group in Phoenix called the Mothers of Twins Club. The meetings were fun and hilarious when others told about their experiences in raising multiple birth kids. One of the problems we had, however, was that we were so busy raising ours we didn't have time to attend the meetings.

Sunday Mass was a real challenge. The six of us would sneak into the back of the church crying room. Beleaguered by the stress of just getting there on time, exhausted by the fact that one or the other had kept us up that night, busy wiping leaky noses and "pitiup," mad at each other for not helping more, annoyed by the missed leisurely breakfast, dedicated to the security of our children, we had trouble with the priest's sermon on conciliatory marriage relationships.

The Pope would never sit in a crying room. "Sorry, Father," I thought, "You are single, you had a leisurely evening with your newspaper and your Bible. You were permitted to sleep all night. You had a good breakfast. You didn't have to chase, scrub, dress, scold, comb and referee four kids in order to get here to this monkey cage. "Et Spiritus, Dominos Hibiscus, to you, too!"

Chris and Theresa "helped" lots with the twins. However, Theresa wasn't daddy's little baby anymore. Quite conversant by age four, she regressed a bit, going back to baby talking to get attention. Chris actually took his daddy to task once, complaining that everything was for the twins. "It's always the twins," he complained, "What about me?" He was right. We had to make a few adjustments. We attempted to center a little more attention his way. He was a great kid.

In 1965, I was finally given a classroom at the college that I could convert into a small animal conditioning lab. The only problem was that there was no money available to buy any equipment. No money for Skinner boxes, no money for electronic relay racks, no money for rats. Just a room and a fellow who wanted to design and stock a lab.

I started out by coercing the college carpenter into the building of nine little booths along the outer wall of the room. I remember how he laughed at me when I requested that the booth counter tops be covered with Formica so that it would be easy to clean up after the animals. "You've got to be kidding," he said, so I painted them with enamel.

I got a small National Science Foundation grant for lab equipment one year that bought a large demonstration conditioning chamber and enough smaller units for five of the booths. The next year I got more. A government electronic surplus supply got me lots of 26.5 volt telephone relays that I incorporated into a homemade master control panel and a complex interresponse-time data collection center (whatever that is?).

The class I offered was Psy 112, the *Experimental Analysis of Behavior*. Students who enrolled attended three hours of lecture each week and had to sign up for the two-week lab that required attendance and participation for a full three hours each afternoon. I had very little trouble getting twenty-seven students to sign up each semester, so with nine booths available, I would offer the lab at three different times. Is it any wonder that I soon became the "rat man" on campus?

Here's an interesting sidelight: I taught Psy 101 classes for the evening college on Mondays and Wednesdays. Lots of very active babies needed lots of shoes. One evening I gave a demonstration of one of my smartest rats performing in the professional chamber. The students watched my animal lever pressing rapidly as I recorded response frequency, the time between the successive responses and the cumulative responding data. All of this was done using panels that were loaded with clicking relays, flashing lights and graphic recorders that automatically drew impressive charts. Even I was impressed!

Later that week, the phone rang in my office and a news reporter was calling from the leading Phoenix news television station requesting an interview and a demonstration of the new laboratory at Phoenix College. An employee of theirs had seen my demonstration in the night class. Not necessarily a publicity hound, I was nonetheless pleased that someone was interested, so I agreed. "We'll send a reporter with a camera. Will 9 o'clock in the morning be all right?" "Sure," I said. And so they did.

Well, guess what day my relay panel developed a short-circuit? When Bill Stull from Channel 12 News showed up with his camera I was caught pulling panels out of my equipment that had taken months to install, trying to eliminate the shorted unit. Bill waited patiently. I was disgusted. When I got up and running, I went into the animal cage room to get my super rat convinced that I would find him dead!

The rat was fine and plenty hungry. He performed for the camera like a pro. Bill shot lots of 16mm film (no video cameras, then) featuring close-ups of "Mickey" pressing levers, pulling chains on command, etc. Then there were the close-ups of the recorders and the flashing lights all tabulating data while I spoke for three or so minutes into a sound recorder explaining the conditioning process demonstrated in the class I offered at the college. Even I was impressed.

On the 10 o'clock news that evening my segment ran a total of thirty seconds. Ray Thompson called the "Dean" of Arizona broadcasting, introduced my performing star and noted that there was something new at Phoenix College. "Don Huard, professor of psychology has developed a lab in which animals are used," etc., etc. I was never on camera. Instead as they showed my rat pressing the levers, my voice came into the background explaining the conditioning process. Just under the white rat, much to my consternation, they printed the words, PROFESSOR DON HUARD!

Now, I can take a ribbing as much as the next man, but I couldn't believe the number of people who saw that newscast and the kidding I took over the next few days. Dr. Hannelly, the president of the Maricopa County Community College District, sent me a memo: "Congratulations, Don! On behalf of the administrative staff of the District I am pleased to honor you for your exemplary performance Thursday evening as seen on the Channel 12 News Ray Thompson Report. You have represented your college with distinction."

You win a few, you lose a few…

Teaching my classes and labs in the 1960s became more difficult. College students across the country turned rebellious, notably, over the Johnson-Nixon War. Those were troubled times and the news was mostly about the boys brought home in body bags. It was nearly impossible to justify America's involvement in Vietnam as far as the potential draftees were concerned.

The rebelliousness carried over into other areas. Drug usage, resistance to the death penalty, police brutality, contempt for the older generation, you can name it. They all resulted in angered expression in the classroom. In the early 70s members of the National Guard shot and killed four young war-protesting students at Kent State University. It was tough standing in front of a college classroom at that time. Those were frightful times.

Once, one of my students all but screamed in anger. "You old people have made such a mess of things. Now we want our turn." I explained that whether or not the youth wanted their turn, it was coming for them, like it or not. They would have to make many difficult decisions that would affect those who followed *them*. For many of those decisions, *they* would not be thanked. They were not impressed by my message. Many were angered even more.

In the late 70s, the war finally over, students became students again. I felt as though I were an authoritative professor again, rather than a battering ram. It was nice. John Ransom, a gentle, fine arts teacher of ours, was standing before a large mural one morning painted by several of his art students. I passed by on my way for coffee. "Admiring their work, John," I asked? "You know," he answered, "it's so nice that at last they are listening again. I can give them the benefit of my experience and not be threatened by their reactions." I was impressed by John's comment. I felt the same way. The wars were over.

During those meanest of times in the late 60s, being a daddy was tough. Being a teacher was tough, too. However, I never regretted my acceptance of a contract at Phoenix College. I was concerned, however, that I had left the University a year or so too soon. Busy as I was, teaching days and evenings, there was still lurking in the depths of my being, the burning desire to complete my doctoral studies. I couldn't get away from that obsession.

After a few years had gone by, time was running out. A candidate is given only five years following the "comps" to complete the dissertation, and I had only a year and a half or so left. How was I going to find the time to get the job done? Would I be able to get a new graduate committee to direct me, since so many of my original committee members were no longer teaching at the University? How would I be received by new faculty members who had little to do with my earlier development?

I was eventually able to reinstate myself in the doctorate program and completed all requirements in 1971.

Chapter Ten

"Welcome Home, Doctor Daddy"

Excited as I was with my new teaching contract at Phoenix College in 1963, I had to consider the potential consequences of leaving the University a year too soon, thereby losing out on an opportunity to complete my doctoral dissertation with my already established doctoral committee chaired by a very capable professor. I told him about my concern before signing the new contract and was told that it was possible to do a dissertation "on the run."

I didn't know that a year later my mentor would take a new job himself at the University of Hawaii, leaving me with the problem of setting up a new committee. The college catalog permitted completion of a dissertation up to five years beyond the completion of the doctorate comprehensive examinations, which I had successfully completed.

To my complete surprise, I was advised that it would be necessary for me to re-take those exams, then complete a critical review paper before I would be permitted to do the dissertation. Just three years had gone by since I left the University, so I felt justified in requesting additional time to complete the dissertation without re-examination. My petition was denied. In as much as it takes at least a year to prepare for "comps," I felt that the requirement for re-examination was unfair, notably with consideration of the fact that I had not left the field and had been teaching during the interim.

I didn't know what to do. At the suggestion of another professor I consulted with the dean of the college of liberal arts about my concern.

I made an appointment with him and was immediately sent to talk to the new acting chairman of the psychology department to request for more time to complete my work *without* re-examination.

I had successfully completed my foreign language requirements, presented my master's thesis at a symposium before the faculty and fellow graduate students and after a year of special study I passed the twelve hour doctorate comprehensive examination that extended over two highly stressful days in 1963.

A little instruction about the nature of a comprehensive examination might be useful at this point. Mine consisted of a two day written exam over four distinct areas of the field of psychology: The history of psychology, the history of the psychology of learning (called conditioning), Behavioral modification techniques in clinical psychology and research design and statistics. After a year of preparation, on Labor Day in 1963 I wrote for seven hours on the first two areas, six hours on the following day. My graduate committee passed me on my writing in all of those areas.

By that time I had acquired some teaching experience at that same University, so I used that reference to gain support. I performed as a lecturer in my own classes often taught in a large lecture hall, including several I taught with more than 140 students.

I recall something that happened one evening at about that time. I told my wife the pressure of teaching and studying at the same time was getting to me. God bless her, she carried much of my frustration as her own. Later in the evening when our four kids were in bed, I saw her standing in the yard out by the kids' swing set. Marie was crying. I put my arms around her and listened to her as she complained about how I had been isolating myself from her for months while I selfishly buried myself in my own problems. "You don't let me in," she cried. And I knew she was right. "Look at what it's doing to *us*. I knew she was right. "I know how much you want to be a doctor, but what is this doing to your family?"

Much to my surprise and delight, "Dr. Bob," (as I will call him) and I got along beautifully. I learned to respect him immensely, not just for the help he gave me, but also because he was so sincere and considerate.

He seemed to be very sure of himself. His cooperative, helpful style, more than anything else, is why I managed to get my degree.

The relationship that was eventually established between Dr. Bob and me was incredible! He was a brilliant mentor, a capable researcher and he was willing to direct my dissertation! He wanted to stress the future as we worked together over the next year.

I spent hours in his office week after week, while he instructed me individually, using his blackboard and chalk, writing out potential research designs and suggesting methods of statistical analyses that would be pertinent to my study. Looking back on it now, I realize what a marvelous experience it was for me. I was getting the opportunity to learn from a most competent professor who was truly intent on helping me fulfill my potential. I was seeing the best of graduate dissertation preparatory training.

We set up a new committee with the doctor suggesting the other four members who might be interested in my project. We held several project design meetings and input from the others helped to strengthen what had become my dissertation proposal. Finally, I had approval of the design and approval of the graduate college of a petition for an extension of time to complete the study.

Because my new study was in the area of language conditioning, not one for animal research, I had to use an experimental procedure that involved short-term conditioning of hundreds of psychology students in dozens of "borrowed" classes both at Phoenix College and at the University. That meant getting the cooperation of other professors, which I was able to do.

I would carry a heavy projector and written instruction sheets, data collection sheets and special pencils to each class to be tested. The thirty-minute procedure was cumbersome at first in the "pilot" studies. Then it became refined and appropriate as a good method for "teasing out" the data needed to test my experimental hypotheses.

I remember a specific day when I raced across the campus carrying a projector and supplies by myself in 110 degree July heat, thinking that I would surely die before the day was over. When I got to the prearranged class, I was so nervous presenting instructions to the students that I could hardly be heard. When it was over, my mentor said, "You have to speak louder, Don." As time went on, my presentations were clearer and smoother and eventually I had all of the data needed.

The data analysis committee meetings were helpful, teaching me some mathematical techniques that I used years later in my own teaching of classes in statistical methods at Phoenix College. Some of those techniques are mentioned in my book *Behavioral Statistics: Methods of Analysis and Persuasion* published by Kendall/Hunt Publishing in 1992.

After months of data compilation and analysis, I was ready for the final write-up of the dissertation and the preparation for its defense before the final examining committee. It was at that time that I began to see the special goodness of Dr. Bob. Two occasions stand out in my memory. I had taken the summer off from my teaching at Phoenix College and the final completion date for my defense was set for August 20, 1971.

One afternoon as I worked feverishly typing my own manuscript (only a foolish candidate does that) in my little cubicle in the department filled with crunched up, throw-away copies of many pages filling the room behind me, the doctor dropped in to see how I was doing. Seeing my tempo and my panic, he paused just long enough to say some magic words to me. "You'll make it, you know," he said. "Stay cool. It's working out fine." He didn't know what those words meant to me at that time. But then, maybe he did…

Another time as I worked on some of the technical graphs needed to illustrate trends in the data, he came in, studied my progress then left for about an hour or so. When he returned he handed me several graphs that he had drawn. As he handed them to me he said, "Here, use these for pages 137 and 138, they will work out just fine."

I was faced with grave family problems at about that time. My father had severe heart problems that resulted in his death. As the oldest son in the Phoenix area, I felt a strong responsibility to be supportive of him and of the rest of the family as we went through that trying time. We all dearly loved our dad and we still do. I remember my sister Shirley asking me on the sad day of the funeral if dad knew I was finishing my doctoral studies. I told her that I had not mentioned it to him because when he was struggling with his own health problems, my little problems seemed rather unimportant by comparison. She suggested, "He knows. He is proud of you."

Doctor Bob was most understanding when I had to be with my family during dad's illness. He was especially kind when dad died.

I missed a scheduled meeting or two and he explained the situation to the other members of my committee. I was so appreciative of his efforts on my behalf. About halfway through the ten-month process, I became aware that my mentor was tuning my head in preparation for my dissertation defense. "If the committee members ask you why you chose the Duncan Multiple Range Test, tell them this," he instructed. Then he told me how to answer lots of questions logically so that I would not get trapped. By the time my defense took place, he had me fine-tuned and even confident that I was in for a very special, very big day with the big boys.

Understandably, I couldn't sleep the night before my special day. The oral dissertation defense was scheduled for two hours at 3 o'clock that Thursday afternoon. Present were my five committee members, another member who was not a committee member and a dean from the graduate college. I had been advised by my professor to present a summary of my research and conclusions over the first forty-five minutes and then I would be questioned for the remaining time.

The title of my dissertation was *The Effects of Stimulus Intensity on the Conditioning of Word Meaning*. Knowing that our "guest" from the graduate college was not familiar with the classical conditioning process basic to my study, I preceded to teach the Pavlovian conditioning paradigm at a very low level as I had done for my own psychology students at Phoenix College. Then, I planned to proceed to the complexities of my research.

I was suddenly interrupted by a question from one of the members. "What makes it work, Don," he asked. I thought a bit, then answered, "I don't know, sir." Out of the corner of my eye, I saw the graduate dean shift in his chair as his facial muscles tightened. Probably, he was thinking, "Oh, oh, this fellow's in trouble!"

However, I pointed out that even Ivan Pavlov himself never provided that answer. "Pavlov said the association was dependent on irradiation across the higher areas of the cerebral cortex, a process he was never able to demonstrate." I added, "In recent research, attempts have been made to correlate these changes with measured changes in RNA, the biological cousin to the hereditary molecule DNA that is said by some to store memory. However, the correlations have never been established."

A most marvelous thing happened. The questioner was completely satisfied with my answer! He smiled broadly, a smile that I interpreted as something like "OK, the candidate is not going to try to snow the members of the committee. He's going to admit what he doesn't know. Now, let's get on with the business of the day."

The business of the day proceeded so smoothly that I could hardly believe it! Soon I was fielding questions just as Dr. Bob had instructed me and it was all working. When I got cornered a little, the professors seemed more amused than concerned. However, at 5:15 P.M. they were still asking me questions and I began to get a little nervous. "Why are they keeping me so long," I wondered. At 5:40, they had me leave the room. After the longest fifteen minutes in the history of the entire world, the door opened and one of them reached his hand out to me saying, "Let me be the first to congratulate you, **Doctor Huard**." I shook hands with the other members, then spied my open dissertation on the desk, topped with all of the signatures I needed for completion.

Of course, after niceties with the dean and the others on the committee, the first thing I did was to go into the office to call my Marie. "It's all over, honey. Now we can start living again." As I walked to my car, feeling a thousand pounds lighter, carrying my precious briefcase as though it contained expensive jewelry, I paused to ask my mentor, "Why did they keep me so long? Don't they have families to get home to," I asked? "They were interested, Don" was the only answer I got.

Before leaving the east end of the valley, I had a special place I was compelled to visit, the Green Acres Cemetery where my dad was buried. There I sobbed out a few years' worth of tension as I shared my success with my father, wishing that he could know how much I missed him and how much I wanted him to be proud of my accomplishment. Again, I could hear Shirley telling me, "He knows, Don. He knows…"

Stopping by in Scottsdale to give mom the news, I came upon a delightful surprise. It seemed warm in the house. Then I realized that my mother had been burning candles in every room in the house! Her whole afternoon had been spent praying that all of those people at the University would be good to her son Donnie. Moms are like that, you know. God bless you, mom. I miss you so much.

The best came last that day. I was exhausted after the stressful examination and the long drive to our home on the west side of Phoenix. I turned off of Camelback Road and into our darkened neighborhood, then turned again onto Elm Street and finally drove up onto our driveway. As I drove into the carport, the lights of my car illuminated a large colorful sign taped to the front of the utility room.

It read: Welcome home, Doctor Daddy!

* * *

Approximately six months after my release from the military in 1954, I began my college studies that were finally completed with my doctorate in 1971. That's a span of seventeen years. I was then forty-one years old. Not being considered as a "brilliant" student, my first years were somewhat remedial in nature. But as the years went by, I became determined to continue advancing in academia.

I learned many things in addition to the formal training needed for my profession. Among them is the fact that persistent determination can result in much achievement in the long run. I learned that wanting something bad enough to go after it with one's heart and soul is a positive thing. Refusal to give up on a dream can pay off in time.

I learned that you don't go to college to "get" a degree. Instead, you must earn it. You have to "build" it. It takes a long time and requires a great amount of self-discipline. The higher you go in academia, the greater the challenge to achieve. Therefore, we feel a greater sense of accomplishment after each successful step along the way.

I learned that there is no such thing as a "self-made" man or woman. Anyone who accomplishes much, owes much to those who helped along the way. No one does it alone.

I learned that there are lots of ways to live a productive life. Early adulthood is a time for investigating options, for finding where we best fit. For most of us, it does not involve higher education. Society needs plumbers, cooks, landscapers, secretaries, machinists, store cashiers and those who stock the shelves, as well as engineers, doctors, lawyers and executives.

The trick is to find where we will best fit in and can be happiest as a person who contributes his or her skills and motivations to making the world a better place. For me, it was in the field of education. I decided to be a teacher. I began teaching at the University as a psychology lecturer at the age of twenty-eight, just after I got my Master's degree. After three years, I was hired to teach at Phoenix College, where I remained as a professor for the next thirty-eight years.

"Welcome home,

Doctor Daddy!"

Chapter Eleven

Babies, Boats, Birds and Bees

It was a bit unusual to have the gentle snowfall in mid-April of 2002 that we experienced then in the beautiful Bradshaw Mountains near Prescott, Arizona. Usually the winter snows end in March, but the season ran late that year. Margaret (my present wife and the mother of my three grown step-children) and I enjoyed our hilltop home in a lovely place that is called Groom Creek, about seven miles from town, out a winding road called Senator Highway, named after Arizona's famous senator, the most Honorable Barry M. Goldwater.

Retired then, we had lots of time to enjoy the mountain atmosphere, the pine trees and the wildlife. It's not unusual to see a few deer roaming near the road on the way into town. We have to watch for them when we drive because they cross highways to get to the lakes for their water. In the summer we see them on our own lot. Javelina, fox, coyote and lots of squirrels roam the area in the mountains near Prescott. Our elevation is a little higher than the mile-high city of Prescott. We are at 6200 feet and so we get a little more snow and a temperature that is usually about five degrees cooler. Best of all, in the summer our average temperature is eighteen degrees cooler than Phoenix.

We love Prescott. We love being away from the hot, busy, confusing congestion of the big city of Phoenix, where we spent our lives raising our families and working. I was a teacher. Margie spent twenty years as an executive secretary for the Greyhound Corporation. We met a few months after Marie passed away in late 1981.

I owe much to Margie for giving me a new life filled with love and devotion and a happier perspective on things after a period of profound sadness. A lesson I have learned through the years is that even the deepest emotional trauma can be followed by recovery and renewed commitment to others, e.g., family and friends. I learned that an overwhelming sense of loss at one time of life, however painful, need not confine any person to endless isolation from the potential for establishing new relationships, even those of a romantic nature.

I don't mean to imply that life with Marie through twenty-three years of marriage and the raising of our four children was, overall, filled with sadness. On the contrary. We had a good marriage with lots of admiration, love, respect for one another and a positively shared commitment to our children, in spite of my often-times costly preoccupation with academic advancement. A bit too serious about life generally, we nonetheless had lots of joy watching the kids grow in our own likenesses, through the good and the bad times we associated with parenting.

There simply is no way to adequately prepare for parenthood. There is no way to realistically assess ahead of time the complex, challenging responsibilities assumed by those who become parents, either by choice or by happenstance. Being a good parent requires an incredible amount of patience, control, self-discipline, tolerance and understanding, all characteristics that are slow to develop, even in those persons with the very best of intentions.

Parenting, therefore, is not for the young. It is not even a good idea for teenagers, almost all of whom are still struggling with their own self-understanding. Maturity takes a lot of time. Good judgment and the ability to guide others and serve as an appropriate role model comes only as a result of much life experience. Even young couples in their twenties find parenthood more challenging than they could ever have imagined.

Marie and I were married in 1959. Just a little over a year later our lives changed considerably as we waited for the birth of our first child. Those were the days when you simply waited for the birth to occur before you found out whether you had a son or daughter. Our sandy-haired son Christopher Leon (after Marie's father) was perfect in every way. His mother fondly called him "Tweeters," a name that didn't stick, but rings fondly in my memory.

Mom was as perfect as her newborn child. It's not likely that any child ever got better care or more love. However, daddy got lots of love too, so in a matter of just a few months we became aware that a second child was on the way. Ideally, having a son as the oldest you would hope for a little sister to follow. Well, we got it right… Theresa Ann was born just one year and two days after the arrival of our son.

From the very beginning we were awed and inspired by the wonder of our children. Now I know that no one is surprised to hear that, but for me, as a young psychologist, there was fascination in everything they did and, especially, in everything they said.

Years earlier I had been enrolled in a class at the University called Developmental Psychology which was child psychology taught by a lady professor clearly in love with every child she had ever known. Toward the end of the class, Mrs. Whitney asked each of her students to observe a child very carefully for a few days and do a write-up of the child's activities for a semester report.

Not being very interested in children during the days of my bachelorhood, I asked for permission from my professor to write something on adult behavior instead. "I'm more interested in grownups," I argued, "not children." Mrs. Whitney thought for a moment, then gave me my answer. "Think, Mr. Huard, about precisely where grownups come from." I thought her logic left much to be desired. After I thought about it, however, my professor seemed to grow intellectually. I did the required assignment.

I knew so much when I was young, that I don't know now. I knew how to be a good parent before I began to learn how difficult it is to be a good parent. I had the cure for so many of society's ills before I began to learn about the complexities of society's ills. Nothing makes us more aware of our limitations than the assumption of parental responsibility. The reason for this is that there is no greater challenge than that of being an effective parent. Fortunately, there is no endeavor that offers greater potential for life fulfillment and reward than meeting that challenge.

So, Marie and I delighted in the development of our kids. As a psychologist interested in language processes, I watched the conditioning principles studied in the classroom and laboratories at the University work on my own children as they learned to understand words and eventually to use them as vocal "tools" for getting what they wanted. I was fascinated with the process called *tacting* which is the naming of objects and the way a child learns to label all things in his immediate environment. Subject to the reinforcement provided by the parents, a child learns the most appropriate labels not only for "mommy," "daddy," "Ginger" (the family dog), but also for "McDonno's" and grandpa's car, "Chebbie-too."

Imagine what it must be like to be a toddler, when just about everywhere you go, you see something for the very first time. The child's language grows exponentially. Subject to parental reinforcement, new sights and experiences result in the assignment of new labels. It becomes a game. "There's Checker Auto," he says. And that's the "Derry Qweeen."

Interestingly, the child's language takes on the tone and the phrases used by his parents. "You got a nuther think commin," they say, just like mom. "Too big fer yer britches," they giggle, just like dad. "Dat's a Pwitty fwower," Theresa purrs, as she looks at the pansies in the neighbor's yard. "I wuv you," they whine at bedtime, melting your insides.

The innocence of a child is special to behold. They sometimes catch you off-guard, when you are unaware that they are watching what you're doing as a parent. "Daddy, why did you tell that man (at the plant nursery as we drove home with a new tree for the front yard) that we had some peat moss? We don't have any peat moss at home." That, from Chris, age four, who wondered why daddy told a lie. "Daddy, how come trees are always hooked to the ground? Could we get a marshmallow tree?"

My earliest awareness of how much my young son was copying my mannerisms as well as my words was pointed out to me by Marie one morning when Chris was not yet a year old. I felt Marie tugging at my sleeve as we ate breakfast with Chris sitting in his highchair near the table. "Look at what he's doing," she whispered to me. Chris had a paper napkin in his left hand and was "scrunching" it as he played with his food. "I've seen you do that dozens of times," she said. "You think he's not watching you?"

Knowing that your child is following your example, whether you are aware of it or not, serves as a startling revelation, making you think that it might be advisable to take a closer look into the kind of person that *you* are. Am I the kind of person I want him to be," I often asked myself? The responsibility to serve as a good role model is awesome, to say the least. Your very being is in the process of transmission to this new little person whose life is every bit as important as your own. The child's personality is a reflection of your own. You must work hard to be a worthy mentor for the most precious of God's gifts, your beloved children.

Our son Chris was always a source of great pride to me. He was adorable to look at, warm and considerate as a child and cute as the dickens in some of the things he did. At age two he would hold his tiny fist in the air in a playful, menacing way and say, "You wanna hit with my socker?"

There are no words sufficient to convey the extent of my love and fondness for my only natural daughter, Theresa. From the first time I saw her, I was lost to the sweetness of this child, a reflection of her mother's love and kindness. Theresa has given my life special grace, from the times that she donned her Easter bonnet and a frilly dress for church on Sunday to the present day when, as a mother of two, Jeremy and Stacia, she still finds much time and love for her own father.

Those days, Theresa and her fine husband Bill (a small engine mechanic) were sincerely interested in everything Margie and I did as grandparents. They seemed to genuinely treasure our involvement in their lives. They listened patiently to us when we told of our experiences raising our own children. We tried to encourage them in times of trial with their own kids, assuring them that they were doing a good job with parenting, especially in view of the fact that both were working so capably in very demanding careers.

Theresa serves as "Executive Editor" for the things I write, such as this book about my family. She's highly skilled in correcting my miscues and unskilled expressions as a result of her work, years ago, in the Linguistics Department at the University of Arizona, her very disciplined, successful training as a court reporter and her many years as a medical transcriptionist working in the Pathology Department of Boswell Hospital in Sun City. I'm especially proud of my accomplished daughter.

How she finds time to help me with my writing, I will never know. How I could have been so fortunate to have her as a daughter, I'll never know. How God must love me, to have given me such wealth!

Chris tried the trumpet once. It didn't take very well. Maybe he should have tried drums. Maybe he would have become a long-haired rockstar. Our daughter did play the clarinet for a year or two. Much of her time was spent in addition to her schoolwork and time for countless friends, in helping mom care for the twins who arrived when Theresa was only about four years old.

Fortunately, Marie and I finally concluded that four kids were enough. At the risk of the potential loss of our eternal souls, we limited our personal activities to the holding of hands for the remainder of our marriage. If you believe this, well…

David and Greg were both the best of buddies and the worst of enemies all through their earlier years. They were almost always together, beginning their days with the first kid awake getting a "free shot" at his sleeping kid brother. Wrestling on the new carpet in the unfurnished dining area of our home in the evening usually ended when one or the other cried "foul!" As soon as one of them got hurt, both were sent to bed. The early riser the next morning would be sure to get even.

In late 1971, the Huard family moved from the west side of Phoenix over to a new home on Laurel Lane in northeast Phoenix. It was a lovely home with four bedrooms, a slump block front and a large pie-shaped cul-de-sac lot with an enormous, unmanageable backyard. The years spent in this home were some of the best that Marie and I had, as I was earning better money then and the kids were growing toward high school age.

I bought a boat. It was the first of several that we "enjoyed" through the next few years. One thing is sure about any boat. The best day is the day you buy it and the second best is the day you sell it. The first one I bought was a fourteen foot open MirroCraft aluminum boat with no motor. Then I bought an old eight horsepower Wizard (Western Auto) motor that had no cover cowling from a boat wrecking yard and tuned it to push us along at a respectable speed.

The boat was designed for a 25 horsepower motor, so we were quite underpowered, but at least we were powered. I paid $200 for the boat and $38 for the motor. I painted a new name on the side of the boat. "Boat."

Chris and Theresa were about, say, seven and six at that time. That's old enough to enjoy some special time with dad at a few of the local lakes. Most of the time Marie stayed at home taking care of the twins while dad and the older kids went to play. I towed the boat on its tiny Dilly trailer with my dad's old Chevy II. We went to Lake Pleasant and Saguaro, Canyon and Apache Lakes with that boat.

Eventually we graduated to a better boat. It was called a Ski and Troll, another aluminum 14 footer but this time with a little blue metal nose deck, a windshield, built in steering and front throttle controls. It was a nice boat, powered by a Sears 25 horsepower twin cylinder engine.

That was the one we once took to a big place known as Roosevelt Lake, where small boats such as ours were better left at home. Dad made a big mistake on that day, putting himself and his older kids in considerable danger. He should have known better. He still trembles a bit to this day just thinking of what could have happened because of his careless miscalculation.

After I backed the trailer into the water and unhooked the boat, we started for the other side of that large lake. The water was smooth and the breeze was gentle under a clear sky. Getting over to the other side took a long time. When we got there we weaved in and out of the coves, enjoying the nice scenery, occasionally getting on shore to skip rocks on the water.

I guess we were enjoying that beautiful morning a little too much. What I didn't realize was that the sky was darkening and the wind was getting stronger as we played. We were on the shore when I first noticed that there was a storm coming and decided that we had better get back to the car. "Come on, kids," I said. "Load 'em up. It's getting a bit rough out there. We had better get back to the car."

When I pulled the rope on the engine, it started immediately. However, the increasing wind was blowing directly into the cove we were trying to exit. It blew the boat against the rocky shore, shearing a shear pin! That's the little brass pin that shears when the engine propeller hits rocks so that you don't destroy that expensive prop. No problem. Any smart boater carries a tin of the shear pins just in case and they are easily replaced.

Out of the boat, I lifted the rear of the engine out of the water, pulled the cotter key, removed the prop and installed a new shear pin. "Now this time I'll push us out farther before I fire up this sucker," I said. "Chris, just steer us straight out of the cove if we get clear."

However, the wind was getting stronger and, guess what, there went another shear pin! On the third attempt we managed to get free of the rocks and headed out across the lake toward the car. About a third of the way across the approximately two miles of water I began to realize that the "sea" was getting very rough and that because we were underpowered we were only very slowly making headway.

I looked around at that time for others on the lake. There was no one. Only the Huard family in their little Ski and Troll, sloshing around in a turbulent sea. It dawned on me that anyone with half of a brain had gotten off of that lake an hour ahead of that storm!

I quickly put on all three life jackets (just kidding). Actually, we all had life preservers on, but it was still a very dangerous situation to be in. And dumb daddy had set it up perfectly! Chris and Theresa were in the front seat, cowering under the windshield, dad was kneeling in the back near the motor, holding onto the front seat and sounding re-assuring as he advised Chris to just head straight into each wave and "we'll get to the other side before you know it."

In the middle of the lake the waves were coming up over that windshield. I was getting drenched. It seemed as though we were getting nowhere. The boat was designed for a 45 horse engine. We were pushing with just 25. At that point I turned around and suddenly I became frozen with fear. My head pounded when a terrifying thought hit me as I looked at that little engine, purring along at about three-quarters throttle, the huge waves slapping loudly against the hull of our boat.

"When was the last time you gassed that engine," I gasped? It hit me that if the tank on the top of that engine were to empty, we would lose power, the waves would turn us sideways, then roll us over. We were in serious trouble…

Boating rules employed by anyone with any sense of caution whatever (excluding guess who?), clearly inform that you never try to fuel a running engine. A spark could blast you away. But, what could I do? Tossing from side to side, buffeted by the fierce wind, I loosened the filler cap. I poured a half gallon of gas from a can into the tank on top of the engine. Most of what I poured sloshed over the running engine and into the boat. Much of it increased the pollution in Lake Roosevelt.

"Thank you, God." The engine did not explode. I collapsed in the back of the boat, feeling very sick to my stomach, however, at least more secure in the knowledge that the engine would keep running. After all, it was from Sears…

After what seemed like forever, we approached the shore near grandpa's old Chevy II. The wind was howling above the huge rocks as we settled into water that was calm at last. Protected from the wind by those rocks, I prayed a thank you to the Lord for getting us to safety. "Oh, Lord deliver," I had prayed, just like Viola said I should. And He did.

About that time, Theresa turned around, looked at me with a complete absence of even the slightest concern and said the strangest thing. "Daddy," she asked, "If I fall into the water, is it okay if I get my hair wet?" You know, I damned near kicked that kid overboard!

Chris, like his daddy, had been terrified. Theresa, bless her heart, had trusted her daddy's assurance completely and wasn't worried. It took me several hours to get my heart rate back to normal. A week or so later, I sold that boat. You had better believe, I give special meaning to the wise words of the Aga Khan (or somebody). "You just don't mess with Mother Nature."

Still, I loved boating, not fishing, particularly, but boating. So it wasn't long before we took on a new project. I was driving home from the college one day and I noticed an old boat sitting on a rusting trailer in an open field. I turned into the area and studied this aging, Arizona sun-baked vessel with its rough, parched mahogany deck and visibly neglected engine. It was a 16 footer, larger than our other boats, with a big four cylinder Evinrude. There was a sign on it requesting $500 or "best offer."

Chris was about ten or so at that time. I was looking for a project that he and I could share. This old boat seemed the perfect answer. In fact, I was reasonably certain I was going to buy it even though I hadn't heard the engine run or even talked to its owner.

Saturday morning Chris and I went over to see that boat. I acted real uncertain as to whether or not I was interested in it and kept asking Chris what he thought. I could see the sparkle in his eyes and could hear the excitement in his voice as he tried to convince me that we could make that old engine run. "We'll put some air in those trailer tires, dad. Then we can tow it home."

The fellow said that the engine was running okay when he just quit using the boat a few years earlier. He said he would take $400 for it. Knowing that I had already decided to buy it, I nonetheless acted unconvinced, then turned to Chris and said, "Well, son, you decide. Do you think we can handle this one?" The boy exploded with excitement. We gave the man the money, took the old wheels over to the service station to put air in the tires and towed our treasure home.

Marie was not too enthusiastic about what she saw as we brought her out to the driveway. However, in a couple of hours and with a garbage can filled with water thinking it was a lake, we had that engine running! It sputtered and puffed, but smoothed out nicely just like my old Beaver when the RPMs were up. I installed a new set of plugs. Fine tuning brought a gentle idle. We were pleased with the super acceleration that emptied the lake onto the driveway.

Next we took the engine off of the boat, the boat off of the trailer and we turned the boat onto its top (windshield removed) on some 2 x 4s so that we could sand down the rusting exterior. In a few weeks the hull had a glistening white enameled finish. Chris and the twins took on the task of sanding the mahogany deck and dashboard. A sealer and a coat of clear polyurethane finish made the boat look real classy. We recovered the seats with new naugahyde fabric and pronounced our boat as seaworthy.

We enjoyed that boat immensely. Even Marie and the twins went with us to the local lakes for our boating picnics. It was an especially pretty boat that ran so smooth. Each of the kids "demanded" a chance to drive it and daddy weakened from time to time, in spite of his better (?) judgment. By then, as a result of our harrowing experience at Lake Roosevelt, safety was the major priority. Chris enjoyed one special day when we invited his friend Tony to go with us.

During a dry spell financially, I sold dad's Chevy II that I loved so much (dad was gone by then and I hated to let that car go). A young teenager came out, drove it and gave me a badly needed $500 for it. I cried a tear or two as he drove it away. A few days later he called complaining about the trouble he was having trying to start it. The battery kept going dead. Then he said something that really bugged me. "I don't know why I bought that junk car anyway," he complained. I yelled into the phone, "You bring it back to me right now and I'll give you your money back." He didn't, but I wished that he had. That punk kid wasn't worthy to own *my* dad's car as far as I was concerned. I always felt that I had let dad down on that one.

Several years later I saw an ad in the *Arizona Republic* for a really neat boat. That was a boat "to die for" as the kids used to say. No more of those little outboards for the Huards. That beauty was a stern-drive 18 foot fiberglass model with an inboard four cylinder Volvo Marine engine. Donnie was a real mariner on that one. I sold my soul to the tune of $2,150 to get that boat and never regretted the purchase. We used it for about two years, nearly wearing it out before I sold it for $2,000.

Towing a boat that large requires a bit more power and skill, so I started buying old Buick Electras of the 1969-71 vintage. They had big 455 cubic inch V8s that were great for long trips and for hauling heavy loads. We had three of four of those cars over a span of about five years. Two of them we wrecked. Marie canceled one by rear-ending a station wagon. Another was destroyed by getting hit from behind (twice within seconds by two different cars) in a blinding sandstorm on our way back from a vacation trip to Disneyland. It was one of those chain reaction accidents that, in this case, involved a half-dozen cars. There were serious injuries, but, not to us. Chris had a minor concussion, but that was probably good for him at his age.

With a bigger boat and a slightly older, enthusiastic crew, we could hit the big lakes. Lake Roosevelt was no problem. Just watch the sky. Lake Powell, at the very top edge of our state, became our favorite vacation spot for awhile. Several times we traveled up river for 53 miles to reach the famous Rainbow Bridge, a natural stone arch that spans a part of the lake for about one hundred yards. The magnificent scenery in and out of the coves with rock walls that are colored in deep brown and reddish colors dazzled our eyes.

On one occasion we rented a motel unit for one night near the lake. A second night we camped out in one of the coves a few miles from the main boat dock, called Wahweap Marina. We pitched a tent and got settled in for the night just as though we were camping in our own backyard. The weather was perfect. After lots of chasing of each other on the shore and watching the sunset, we crowded into the tent as the batteries on the flashlight burned out. It got darker and darker and darker.

It got colder than we expected. The ground was harder than I expected. We missed our bathroom! I would have traded that boat for a cup of coffee. Then Chris helped a bunch by suggesting to Theresa that there were cougars in the Lake Powell Mountains.

After what seemed like about a week full of hours of freezing restlessness, the sun finally started to appear over on the other side of the lake. In a semiconscious daze, attempting to massage arthritic bones into mobility, I started counting heads. One was missing! We found Theresa asleep way up under the deck of the boat, where she thought she would be safe from the cougars.

We burned out our first transmission driving home from that "vacation." Apparently, the boat was too heavy even for a big Buick

Electra. As we neared Flagstaff, the transmission began to slip and smoke. Then we found that we were not able to climb the hills up into town so I had to find a way to get the boat towed by someone else.

It was getting dark on the road and we were slipping along only very slowly in a lower gear when we came upon a little community with a little bar with a few trucks out front. Leaving my family in the car I went inside and talked a pool-playing good ole' boy to tow the boat up to Flagstaff with his pickup for $20 which he undoubtedly spent that night on booze. We followed in the smokin' Electra.

I got another brilliant idea as I thought about our problem in the cheap motel that night. "Flagstaff is higher than Phoenix, right?" I thought, "Therefore, it must be downhill and maybe we can make it home. Early the next morning I poured more fluid into the leaking transmission and we smoked our way through Flagstaff (I remember seeing the pedestrians coughing) and got only about five miles out of town before that Electra completely expired. We had melted every one of those 455 cubes!

We made it as far as the little park at Fort Tuthill, five miles south of Flagstaff. "What to do, what to do," I pondered. How do I get my family, a dead car and a two-ton boat to Phoenix? Taking little seven-year-old David with me and leaving Marie, Chris, Theresa and Greg in the park, I (we) hitchhiked back into town and went to the Valley National Bank. David enjoyed the ride in a BMW.

At the bank I checked out $500 on my Visa, then David and I began shopping the car lots for a very used car with a trailer hitch. After about four hours and much frustration, we found a dealer with a high mileage Oldsmobile, suitably powered, but with no hitch. The price: $495. Another good ole' boy way out in the sticks put a cheap, but strong hitch on it for me and we headed back for Marie and the kids. It was just getting dark as we arrived.

My family must have wondered who that strange fellow was, driving up to them in that white Olds. "Where did you get *that*," Marie asked? We hooked the boat to the hitch, transferred our gear and drove home to Phoenix. After spending the day wondering where David and dad were, Marie liked that idea.

The next day, Chris and I rented a tow bar and went back up to retrieve the Buick which became the third one I sold to a wrecking yard. Happily, I grew too old for any more boats.

Chris advised me the other academic year that it was on that trip up to get the Buick that he learned daddy's rendition of the birds and the bees. "I was a captive audience in that car as you explained it all to me, dad, at 70 miles per hour."

Oh, the joys of parenthood! How happy I am that it is the kids' turn at raising their own. It serves them right for what they put us through. Or, was it me, who put *them* through it all? Poor Marie. She came along for the ride. I'm glad she did.

Boating "Daze"

Boats we loved

1970s

One burned-out Buick   I wonder why…

Chapter Twelve

Emphasis:

Some say that it is tougher to raise a teenage daughter than it is to raise a teenage son. But what about raising a teenage daughter and three teenage sons? And what if two of the teenage sons are highly competitive twins? Of course, there are lots of families that are much larger, but ours was surely big enough. There were enough experiences for us through the kids' troublesome teenage years to last a lifetime.

Chris spent much of his early teenage years attached to *Gilligan's Island*. He couldn't wait each day to get home from school to turn on the TV for his fantasy overdose. Only with considerable reluctance did he let anything about life interfere with what was important.

Theresa's life revolved around her friends. There were about four young girls in and out of our place on a regular basis. Lisa, Candida, Barb, Marla and others seemed to spend every day engrossed in the world of noisy chatter. They chatted at school, on the way home from school and on the way to the telephone where they would chatter some more.

Mom and dad became her own private secretarial staff. The phone rang constantly and almost always had a young lady attached to the other end dedicated to driving us out of our minds! There is simply no limit to the number of topics that require analysis and evaluation by any teenage girl. Naturally, the number one topic is boys.

After awhile, the constant ringing of the phone became so bothersome (to say it kindly) that I decided that Theresa just had to have her own separate phone, to be answered only by her and only if she would advise her friends that "our" phone was off limits. That didn't work like a charm...

When lady pristine wasn't home her phone would ring and ring, then, after a pause, our phone would ring with someone on the other end wondering why Theresa didn't answer her phone. Soon we were ignoring the ringing of our phone if it was preceded by the ringing of her phone, much to the consternation of those trying to reach *us*.

Chris, David and Greg complained bitterly about the special consideration given to our daughter. "There's only one of her and there's three of us and we don't have a phone," they complained. Finally, I arranged for a third phone to be set up in David's room for the boys who then fought over who should use it when.

"David's always talking on the phone and I hardly ever get to use it," Greg would complain. This was actually true. David talked to girl after girl in the middle of the night and off and on all day, serving as counselor to all of the local heart-broken "foxes" who were being misunderstood by their boyfriends and their parents.

Then, there was the "stereo" problem. For a teenager, there are only two volume settings on a boom box. Off and LOUD! There's nothing in-between, just as there seems to be nothing in-between the ears that listen to it. Guitars sound as if they are in the agony of being strangled. Drums are beaten to death rather than played. "Baby, baby, baby, baby," seems to define the intellectual limits to the language skills of the top ten vocalists of the day.

Once, I served as a faculty counselor and advisor for a fraternity group on the Phoenix College campus. It was an extra-curricular assignment that I really didn't want so much that I tried to get the fraternity disbanded. Well, it wasn't quite that bad, but how could I advise the group when its president, vice president and secretary were all about to be expelled from school because of their poor grades?

They decided that they wanted to have a "dance" in the college gymnasium. "Okay," says I. "I'll talk it over with the dean." As a former drag racer and an airplane mechanic, I was really up on those things...

The evening of the dance, I put on my best suit and served as a chaperone for several hundred teenagers recruited from high schools all over the area who were overstimulated with spastic energy that astounded my imagination. "Not any daughter of mine," I thought, as I scouted the grounds outside for lovers and pot smokers.

I was not prepared for a rock concert. The musicians my fraternity "brothers" had hired looked like a gaggle from Borneo. Nothing anyone looked like matched anything any other one looked like. Some of them looked like they had been smoking their own braids. And they were LOUD! Tone boxes (we used to call them speakers) shook the gymnasium bleachers. The noise was unbearable for anyone over twenty-five years of age, which included me and a couple of other teachers dumb enough to be there at that time.

Any parent who saw those kids doing their premarital jiggling to that deafening voodoo beat would have wanted the faculty arrested. Eventually, at near 10:30 or so, the musicians had so exhausted their instruments that they left, only to be replaced by another group more depraved-looking than the first. Of course, they were even noisier.

I found myself spending more and more time outside, not because I cared if the whole campus was inflamed by pot-heads, but because I was desperate to get away from anticipated damage to my one remaining eardrum.

The gym was jammed with kids, all having a ball. Some were crouched in the corners and under the bleachers for their own extra-curricular activities. I began to get concerned. "What if a cigarette is dropped on the paper that lines the floor of this basketball court," I questioned? "What if a fight breaks out between two boys who have the "hots" for the same girl?"

It was quite late. I looked around for the other chaperons and discovered that Dean Carson had gone home. Benny Aviantos, the P.E. coach, had been smart enough to leave the scene before his brains got scrambled. Then it hit me, "Donnie, you sponsored this thing. You are the only person over twenty-five amidst this jiggling jungle and if anyone gets hurt or the gym burns down, you are going to hang by your thumbs forever..."

A most marvelous thing happened at about 1:00 o'clock the next morning. One of my sub-par fraternity students asked me if I thought that we had better end the "dance." I would have said, "Yes," three hours earlier if I'd had *my* way. He slowly raised the gymnasium lights to a pre-passion level and, to my delight, hundreds of kids just quietly disappeared into the night. It was over, all had survived, even me.

As I drove home in the wee hours I wondered why I had gone into such a near panic, worrying about all of the things that could have happened that didn't. "After all," I thought, "it was just a big bunch of reasonably good kids having a good time, hurting no one. Tomorrow is another day." Perhaps the ringing in my ears would be gone in a year or two.

So it is in dealing with the teenage problems in most families. As parents, we spend too much time worrying about all of the things that could happen that don't. We spend an awful amount of time thinking that our teens have gone bad when they haven't. We have a tendency to overreact. They are mostly great kids. Ours have definitely been great kids. They are just noisy, disorganized, at times inconsiderate, TV - shopping mall - passion over-dosed kids who want a little too much freedom before they are ready for it. It's the parents' responsibility to see that they don't get all of what they ask for. Even the great Garth Brooks says, "Thank God for unanswered prayers."

Moms and dads don't understand what it's like to be young. They don't understand how important it is to own a skateboard and jeans that are so baggy that they can't hold up a wallet! Teens have to be like other teens. That's a very important concept. They would rather be dead than different. They want everyone in the world to know how miserable they are, but they don't want anyone invading their privacy.

Just try to get a teenager to tell you what's wrong. "Nothing," they mutter so low that you can't hear it, then they amble off with their chins near the floor. Mom and dad are seen as the last people who would understand about heartache. Therefore, why bother trying to communicate with them? Meanwhile parents, good luck, as you try to gain a little understanding.

Early in 1981, I received an interesting letter from Loyal Meek, Editor of the *Phoenix Gazette*, the big afternoon newspaper for central Arizona. "Would you like to write a bi-monthly column for the editorial page of the paper under the title *"Emphasis"* as a guest feature writer?" I, and a few others, would be given a special opportunity to express our ideas, concerns, etc., each time with a 700 word unedited (except for spelling and punctuation) column about anything we chose as a topic.

It's most flattering to be called upon by the editor of your favorite newspaper to write your own opinions. After all, my opinions are important. Just ask me how much. I was sure that a million or so readers all over Arizona would be glued to my every word, just as I will undoubtedly have a massive readership for this significant societal contribution.

I simply couldn't resist. I had a great time writing eight editorials over the next year and a half, until they felt that they had heard enough from me. They even put my picture in the paper with each column. Talk about an ego trip! *"Emphasis,"* by Donald Huard, wise counsel of the Universe… I couldn't resist writing about my teenagers:

Emphasis: *The Phoenix Gazette*

Surviving our teenagers -
It just takes a little understanding

By Donald Huard, Professor of Psychology
at Phoenix College

Nobody told us when our twin boys were born in 1965 that eventually they would become teenagers. And now for us, there's no escape. We don't want to complain, understand, but we keep asking why it is that in order to provide a reasonably comfortable home for our kids, we have to be so miserable.

We've already survived two; they are nearly grown. But, these last two are about to do us in. Why, if there are only two of them and there are two of us, do we feel so outnumbered?

For the teenager the stereo is to shout over. No 15-year-old has yet discovered that a volume knob works in two directions. And the bigger the woofers, the better. When their friends are over, the noise is unbearable. A deafening throb that serves as stimulation for weird spastic premarital gyrations they call "groovin." What we used to call "hand-jive, now includes the whole body. They don't just listen to the melody, they "feel the vibes." Whatever happened to music?

There are a lot of things a teenager wouldn't be caught dead in. These include almost all of the things their parents have. Short hair, polyester shirts with buttons, a quiet car and a job. All of these are symbols of the over-the-hill set. For them, it's expensive velour shirts (dad pays for them by wearing cheap polyester ones with buttons), strangulation jeans and shoes with Nike stripes and truck treads.

Teenage boys spend a great deal of their time in a horizontal position, four feet above the sidewalk, impressing their girlfriends by thrashing the air with their feet while making strange oriental noises.

Teenagers hate talking to anyone unless it's by telephone. Avoiding mom and dad if possible they proceed to satisfy their insatiable need for self-expression by chattering into the wee hours with their friends. Almost never are they off of the telephone. One of our boys began to develop mandibular syndrome, a painful affliction involving a serious misalignment of the lower jaw. No expensive surgery required; we cured it by grounding him from the use of the telephone for a few weeks.

Sometimes they do talk to their parents, but only when they feel devilish and are bored with eating, or maybe they need a ride to the mall where they can check out the foxy chicks or see an R-rated movie that we think they can't get *into. They love showing their independence by shocking us with pronouncements like "Don't worry about me over the weekend, mom. I'll be shackin' up with that sweet widow lady down the block."*

A 15-year-old's sense of selective awareness is the wonder of any parent. He is unable to see his dirty socks on the floor in front of **Mod Squad** *day after day, but can look almost directly into a blazing summer sun and see a Dairy Queen sign 5,000 yards away to quote you the price of a frosty slurp, jumbo size.*

He can't see the color beige. Clearly that's where the blind spot is in the eyes of most teenagers. They can't see anything the color of dirt. Earth tones, to most kids, are the erotic sounds they hear coming from their favorite rock groups.

Teenagers always cook twice what they can eat. There is never any interest in rediscovering the remains of yesterday's efforts. Periodically, therefore, the parents find month-old crystalized donuts hidden deep in the refrigerator next to bowls of chip dip and refried beans that are so old they are growing fur. They will use half of anything they open.

Most kids know that if they do anything well, they will be asked to do it again. So they're terrible at chores. Parents get so frustrated trying to get them to work that they just do all of the chores themselves - usually muttering something about hoping that their kids have lots of kids. "It'll serve them right. I hope they have triplets, one set after another before they figure out what is causing them."

Our boys thrive on TV shows that feature screeching tires, crashing cars and noisy black and white cruisers chasing the bad guys with sirens blaring 'Eee-ohh-eee-ohh-eeeee-ohh! I've heard so much of this lately that when I heard an ambulance siren as I drove to work the other day I found myself checking my rearview mirror to see if I was being followed by my television set.

I've become convinced that there are no normal teenagers, only abnormal ones that are like all the rest. I suppose we'll survive them… if only we can develop just a little understanding.

I'm not sure just when I first became aware of the fact that the mother of my children was getting seriously ill. I do remember feeling some special concern years earlier when, on one of our trips to Lake Powell, we went out for dinner at the Wahweap Lodge Restaurant at the lake marina. We had delicious shrimp dinners as a special vacation treat that evening.

There was a band playing country western music and we watched the people enjoying themselves as they danced. I tried to get my daughter to dance with me but she was too shy. "Let's let the kids see mom and dad dance," I suggested to Marie. When we got onto the dance floor and began to move to the music I became very aware that something was wrong with my wife's movement and sense of balance. I remember a deep sadness coming over me. I remember worrying through the next day about something being wrong, but I said nothing at that time.

I knew that my wife had never fully recovered from a stroke that she had when the kids were a few years younger, perhaps still in their grade school years. She was hospitalized for a week or so at that time after suddenly losing feeling and control of the right side of her body. She also suffered from slurred speech and frightening mental confusion. Fortunately, as the days went by, her speech returned to normal and the confusion subsided, but the neurological damage of what the doctors called a cerebral occlusion (arterial blockage) was serious enough to have lasting effects.

Marie and I met on a dance floor at a TGA (To Get Acquainted) dance many years earlier. She danced smoothly and on one great evening we actually placed as runners-up in a waltz contest. However, we hadn't danced since our dating days and the evening at the marina happened when our children were in their teens. Even though I knew that her recovery from the earlier trauma was not complete, I nonetheless was stunned that evening when I suddenly realized how much coordination she had lost and how she was struggling to dance as smoothly as she could.

Through the next few uneasy years we adjusted as a family to Marie's illness, through the bad times, followed by better times, through sad times again, through many hospitalizations and countless visits to the doctor's offices, always in hope of some new treatment that would keep us together as a family. It was not to be. We lost our precious lady in November of 1981.

There is no way that a person can adequately prepare for the loss of his or her spouse. Even with doctors telling me that her condition was "grave" and that they were doing all that they could and that there was little hope, I was still not facing the sad fact that our life together would soon be over. When it was, for awhile, I couldn't face that either, except for one thing, the strength and the love I received from my children and others in my own and in Marie's families.

Today, as I think about and write about those sad times during the last few years with Marie, I prefer to emphasize the positive aspect of our relationship and our shared love rather than the struggles of dealing with her advancing illness. At the funeral, I could think only of the remarkable sweetness of Marie when she was my lovely bride, then the gentle, loving mother of our children long before the onset of her sickness.

It is still troubling and sad to me. I often think of the things that Marie had to miss that I now enjoy. Included are the fulfillment and pride I experience in seeing the children as grown, mature adults. Marie was never even granted the opportunity to behold her own grandchild, as I have done so many times. It's difficult to understand God's purpose in the denial of those treasures. Yet, if one is to believe, then purpose there must be. Marie will be missed and always be loved by her entire family.

I have found new love in my life. It is in my special marital relationship with Margie, a gracious lady who renewed my life, making it rich once again with meaning, closeness, mutual respect and companionship. I would never have thought this to be possible again after a time of such overwhelming sadness. Perhaps this, too, fulfills God's purpose. Perhaps a greater appreciation of the value of what God has given to us comes from the memory of what has been taken away.

When I learn of the way in which some men mistreat their wives I wonder if they realize how unworthy they are of the ones they abuse. Obviously they don't. So they go on from day to day getting so much less out of their marriage than they could because they are building resentment instead of trust.

<u>*Emphasis:*</u>　　　*The Phoenix Gazette*

For Marie -
something special at Phoenix College

By Donald Huard, Professor of Psychology
at Phoenix College

Marie loved Phoenix College. Not because it's a place that is so grand or so spacious, but because, for her, it was so comfortable just being there. To her it was always like Sunday afternoon at the park, warm and filled with people who enjoyed the campus, except at final exam times.

She could be seen trudging slowly across campus each day, heading late for her classes, carrying two large tote bags overflowing with textbooks and too many novels, thick ones that she had extracted from the library. I told her so many times that because of her handicap and the difficulty she had walking that a single bag with less to carry would be better. But she treasured her books. She wanted them with her everywhere she went.

The ladies at the library must have been amused by the way Marie would get so involved in a sad story she was reading that she would cry unashamedly, to the embarrassment of others studying for exams.

Some days, after I dropped her off at the south end of the campus near the library I would worry all day about whether she was all right. I knew she was with friends and if she had any problems someone was sure to call me right away. They're good about that at Phoenix College.

*Often exhausted by an illness that slowly dragged her down, Marie insisted on showing up for all of her classes. She would stay in them as long as she could. She was fascinated by her teachers. "Dr. Van Sittert has so much energy," she would say. "My home-ec teacher is **one terrific lady!** Dean Carson is the greatest. He tries to help those of us who have trouble getting around."*

Many semesters ended at midterm for Marie because her energy ran out. Often, she had to be hospitalized. But, my lady couldn't be kept away.

One sad October afternoon I found her crying at the door of the elevator downstairs from my office. She had been to several classes, then had walked slowly from the other end of the campus and tried to come up to see me. She looked so tired, was unable to muster up the strength to turn the elevator key. Couldn't possibly have climbed the stairs. I took her home, then to the hospital the next day. She was there 19 days before she died. She was just 49.

Marie was not a faculty member, she had no degrees. She's not entitled to have any scholarships awarded in her name. But she was a part of Phoenix College because she was a part of me and that's where I worked. She was one of the many handicapped students who found very special consideration there. She loved the campus, her teachers and me. I was her favorite.

We worked together for many years, getting me through the Ph.D. program at the University. It wasn't easy to raise four kids and handle that hassle at the same time. Not for my wife, not for me. She complained so little, considering the cost. But she accepted the fact that it was what I wanted. I will be forever grateful to her for that.

I hope my readers will understand why, for just this one time, I am permitting myself the indulgence of expressing what's in my soul. Hopefully, no one minds that our youngest son Greg and I planted a rose tree on the campus near the library. With white flowers for Marie. They do that for people who die, you know. Someone plants a tree in a national forest. It's a simple thing, but it's a good idea. It makes you feel just a tiny bit better about things.

But for Marie it's not good enough. She needs... no, I guess her teacher husband needs to see something of her closer to home. Maybe when I walk over to the library on a bright sunny day that tree will be flowering. Maybe I'll see it filled with roses, reminding me of Marie, that dear, sweet lady who was so happy when she was slowly walking along each day, usually late for her next class.

I know that Phoenix College has lots of roses on campus. In the spring it's a lovely place to be. But there is only one rose tree. Surely, the flowers on it will be very special.

Something very special, just for our Marie.

Chapter Thirteen

"But Daddy, That's Different!"

Theresa fell in love in the early part of 1981. It was a somewhat disturbing turn of events for her parents who had only one daughter to be concerned about while they were also trying to keep their three sons under control. Theresa was eighteen and had moved to Tucson where she had a small apartment and a job at the University of Arizona in the Linguistics Department. She was developing all sorts of typewriting and literary skills helping in the production of highly specialized, scholarly books written by the language professors.

After Theresa moved out of Phoenix, Marie and I went down to see how she was doing and to bring a few things for her apartment. Poor girl, she had almost no furniture, not even a TV. She knew only a few people. Her funds were very limited. We helped her as best we could, but she was determined to make it on her own. She always had the very best of intentions.

I sneaked away while she visited with her mother and located a Kmart store in the neighborhood where I purchased a small television set for her. It was only a 15-inch black and white set. I recall having to buy it on my Visa card. Dad was a white knight in shining armor when he returned to the apartment with that set. Little did I know at that time that there was another knight just around the corner in the same apartment complex who would soon displace daddy as the number one man in her life. His name was Bill.

Over the next few months whenever our daughter came to visit us in the big city, her conversations were filled with glowing words about this new fellow whom we had not met. He was handsome, bright, sweet, sincere, and just about everything else great that a person can be when at last you have found the right one after all of your high school years of searching. But Theresa was young and as concerned parents we expressed words of caution that we knew would not be heard.

The big meeting of the minds was arranged. Theresa and Bill would come to Phoenix so that Bill could meet "Big Daddy" and his wife. Poor Bill, it must have been a rough trip. However, Marie and I met this very nice young man, not at all the monster we feared, and we liked him immediately. He was handsome, bright, sweet and sincere, just as she said he was. But then, Theresa always had good judgment with respect to men. After all, wasn't her room always filled with pinups of Andy Gibb? And just consider who she chose as her dad...

At that time, Chris was in an apartment of his own in Phoenix. He was starting a career at the Tip Top Nursery, where he worked his way up to a management position over the years. Marie's illness had gotten worse by then, requiring repeated hospitalizations. It was an extremely difficult time.

There were other things to consider. I must admit that Theresa's planned wedding was not given the consideration that any father should give to an only daughter's special day. In retrospect, I regret that she was not given a church wedding with lots of bridesmaids and a big limo long enough to carry them all.

The wedding was in June, on the 13th, the same date for our wedding in 1959. It was a small wedding, taking place in our new home in Paradise Valley. The preacher was late, the bride was nervous and poor Bill was a basket case. Dad was the cake deliverer, the flower orderer, the photographer, the preacher subsidizer and the father who reluctantly gave away his most precious daughter. Dad and mom were a bit teary-eyed, as dads and moms are supposed to be, when Mr. and Mrs. William Lentz left us with our three boys filling their faces with unused wedding cake. And the house was so quiet.

Marie was gone only five short months later. It's good that she lived long enough to see her daughter's wedding. The wedding seemed to brighten her attitude and mine as well for awhile. Something positive, romantic and alive to take us away from the stresses of her illness, if only for that short while. She left us in November.

We tried to make the best of Christmas. I tried to cheer the kids up. They tried to cheer me up, but with mother gone, it would never be the same. That lovely new Paradise Valley townhome changed from a lovely home into just a house. Marie was everywhere, but not there anymore. The twins could go off with their friends. I stayed at home, taking care of them and trying to take care of myself. Even the fire in the fireplace seemed cold. When I couldn't stand the loneliness, I went to movies that I hardly saw and wandered around the malls noticing all of the couples holding hands. Thank God for work and for lots of understanding Phoenix College students.

Recently, I reviewed some letters I sent to my family and friends over the years following the loss of Marie. One written to Shirley and Joe about three months after Marie's death seems to reflect my changing attitude as I adjusted:

> "As I think back on the loss of Marie I become more aware of the passage of time - time to let the painful immediacy of loss dissipate. It's really rough for awhile, there's just no easy way to adjust. But there is also no appropriate thing to do, but adjust. Only a few weeks after Marie died, Ray suggested to me that I shouldn't try to force anything until I felt the time was right. I guess he was saying that I should give myself time to be sad - as much time as I needed. Then, when I was ready, I would rebuild.
>
> It was good advice.
>
> One day I was standing at the gravesite, still overwhelmed by the loss of what seemed to be everything that was important in the world to me. I was not a complete person anymore. Marie and I had fought a long

and hopeless battle and we had lost. I was alone and a great portion of me had died. You can't believe how old I felt. It was as though we had lived a whole lifetime and it was now over.

As I stood there I noticed another man a little older than me sitting on the ground next to another grave. He was sobbing. He told me about how he had lost his wife a few months earlier and he said he came to be with her every day.

I told myself right then and there that I would not dedicate myself to that kind of chronic emotional trauma. I didn't know what I was going to do to get hold of myself, but I knew from that morning on that the answer was not at that cemetery.

As you know, it didn't take me very long to begin living again. To this day I am comfortable with the knowledge that I did everything I could and that my rather quick recovery from loss need not in any way diminish the meaning of my love for Marie.

I think about her very frequently, but usually in a positive way, the more painful memories being less poignant with that passage of time. I don't try to forget. I don't want to. But I have adjusted. And she will always be special.

I've learned that no part of life is guaranteed permanent. Not jobs, locations, objectives nor even human relationships. So it's best to reach out and enjoy when given the opportunity. We should appreciate the relationships we have, however long they last.

And when they are gone we are wise if we can reconcile ourselves to the undeniable fact that no true love ends happily. It's too bad, but that's the way it is.

If there is any answer at all to dealing with the painful experiences of the past it's in the discovery of the promise of the future. It's difficult to look forward and backward at the same time. After a reasonable time for sadness there's no shame in letting the past be, and looking ahead for new experiences and potential fulfillment.

The real challenge is in learning to put all of these things in some reasonable perspective, resulting in a life philosophy that is positive, forward-looking, productive and emotionally comfortable.

I hope you folks will forgive me if this letter has been a bit too philosophical. Being a teacher makes one a bit too reflective, sometimes a bit too preachy.

One evening in early March of 1982, my younger brother Ken and I were talking on the telephone about being lonely and the difficulty of establishing new relationships. Ken was alone at that time as well. He told me that he had been going on Friday evenings to a place on North 7th Street for meetings and dancing with members of a group called *Parents Without Partners*. I had never heard of the organization which had chapters nationwide. "You might meet someone nice," he advised. The thought of attending even an orientation meeting terrified me.

I thought about it for several weeks, then one Wednesday evening I found myself driving my Buick back and forth in front of the place, trying to get up nerve enough to go in and meet some new friends. David and Greg had cheered me on.

They said I looked nice in my cheap leisure jacket of chocolate brown. I was reminded of the days when I was sixteen, driving up and down the street in front of some sweet thing's house, scared to go get her for a date because I was afraid I might not impress her old man. Or, even worse, that I might. But there I was, fifty years-old, not sixteen!

Finally, after a few near misses, I wheeled my car into the parking lot, got out before I could think about it and went inside. As you might expect, the people were really very nice. Most were divorced people, some were like me, widowed, and all had children and the need to meet people like themselves.

Soon the orientation meeting began. Man, was I uncomfortable… I wanted out of there, to be sure. Then I noticed that there were about ten or so new people just like me who had come to learn about the social activities sponsored by the organization. The fellow who ran the meeting was perfect for the job. He was warm, friendly and funny and had us all reasonably relaxed in no time.

Then came the part I dreaded. "Perhaps you folks would let us know a little about yourselves," he suggested. The microphone was then handed from one of us to the next.

Now, a psychologist has a special problem in settings like this. You see, when ladies find out that you are one of those "shrink-types" they shy away from you as though you have scurvy. I know that many times in subsequent weeks when I would dance with somebody, she would be okay when I told her I was a teacher. If she asked what I taught and I said I was a psychology professor, I could actually feel her back away from me as if I had become a threat to her. One actually said fearfully, "Oh, you're going to psychoanalyze me?"

Knowing this, before the microphone got to me, I devised a plan. No one needs to know I'm (gasp) a psychologist. I stood up when my turn came, introduced myself as Don Huard, a widower with four kids, two (twin boys) still at home and a teacher. I got ready for the next question. "What do you teach, Don," the warm, friendly, funny fellow asked? "I'm in the laboratory sciences," I answered cleverly as I sat down.

"Whew," I thought. "Got through that one. Nobody knows my dark secret." Then, a young thirtyish woman on the other side of the table announced, "I know Dr. Huard. He's a psychology teacher at Phoenix College where I used to go. He was *my* psychology teacher. Hi, Dr. Huard." There went my cover!

I guess it didn't matter that I was exposed. I actually had a nice time that evening in spite of myself and my fears. A nice fortyish year-old very lovely lady actually kept reappearing at my side to talk. It must have been that leisure jacket. I watched a young couple who excelled at the country two-step and thought, "I could learn to do that." I tried it and discovered that I was awful. But, at least I tried.

It cost me $20 for that evening's festivities because after the orientation I signed up for a year's membership. This, in spite of the fact that I wasn't sure I would ever be in that hall again. The lady who took my money seemed nice. Her name was Margaret and she had brown curly hair and pretty blue eyes.

That Friday evening I went back, "just to watch the people dance." Before long I was lumbering through a crude two-step. One lady reappeared and we became friends. We danced some more. Another teacher in her thirties caught my fancy. She was tall, quite attractive, in her late thirties and had two kids attending Shadow Mountain High School like my boys. I really impressed her not at all. Our chemistry was clearly inorganic. Oh, well…

There was a lady in her late sixties who wanted to grandmother my twins. Then there was that lady with the curly brown hair and pretty blue eyes who registered me in as a member. I think she said her name was Margaret.

It took me half an evening to ask Margaret to dance. I had to work up a little confidence first. I would listen to the music fully one-third of the way through before I could decide if it was too fast or too slow or if a two-step would fit for someone with my two left steps. If I couldn't hack it, then at least the music was nearly over.

Margaret struggled with me through one number and we both actually survived. A few more rounds at the two-step, one with grandma and I was ready to call it an evening. When I left I was rather satisfied with myself. It was a nice feeling. I knew I would be back again. "Maybe there's hope for me," I thought.

When I got home reality set in once again. The boys were asleep. It was so cold in the house. I missed my wife so much. It was almost unbearable. "Will this pain ever go away," I asked myself. "How do people like me ever get over these things? What am I doing, going to these dances so soon? I'm so confused about everything."

One evening I danced with Margaret several times amidst dances with that mostly reluctant inorganic chemist and a few others. I learned that Margie (she said she preferred that) was a secretary who worked at the Greyhound Towers right near the Phoenix College campus. To my delight, while we were dancing I told her (what the hell) that I was a psychologist and she was not the slightest bit affected. She didn't care if I was one of those "spooks" or not. I was even in for a special surprise later in the evening.

At about 10:30 that evening Margie came from way over on the other side of the hall, directly to me and announced that she had to leave early because of a heavy work schedule the next day. "Perhaps I'll see you next time," she said. Then she was gone.

I was so taken by that little bit of special kindness shown to me that when I arrived at the hall on the next Friday evening, I saw no one there except for Margie. Sure enough, there she was collecting dues at the table near the door.

She waved when she saw me. It must have been disappointing to her that I was not wearing my leisure jacket. I wore a light blue sweater that Judy had given me for Christmas. I was feeling a little younger, I think.

That was the evening that one lady was down in the dumps. Her kids were giving her a rough time and her ex-husband was being like a monster. She had made herself a bit tipsy and Margie was afraid to let her drive home. So we all took her to a local restaurant for coffee and a nice chat about our kids and other important things. It was there that I really began to study Margie. And I liked what I learned. I liked her calm, self-assured manner, neither too forceful nor too reticent, just nice.

At the next dance I asked Margie if she would consider accepting a dinner date with me. For me, that was one giant leap for humankind! When she said yes, I went into a near panic. Like Michael Douglas in the film *The American President* when he dated Annette Benning, I was a bundle of nerves for that date. "Go for it," the kids said.

Our first date was for dinner at the Black Angus Restaurant. Of course dumb Donnie didn't make a reservation, so the wait for a table was going to be about an hour and a half. "Do you happen to like Mexican food," I asked? "Do I ever," said she, so we ended up over at Jimmie's for enchiladas. After that we saw a movie, Harrison Ford's *Raiders of the Lost Ark*.

It was a most pleasant evening. I learned about Margie's family, including the three kids she had raised essentially by herself after a divorce many years earlier. They were grown and out so Margie was alone in her own home in West Phoenix. I learned that she had worked her way from the secretarial pool at Greyhound all the way up to being an executive secretary for a vice-president of the corporation. Hers was a demanding position and I could tell she was an exceptionally sharp lady who managed her responsibilities quite well.

There was a problem. Margie was accustomed to attending the services at the North Phoenix Baptist Church on Sundays, whereas I, a negligent heathen, couldn't seem to again get comfortable in a wooden pew. Margie seemed to understand, but I think I disappointed her a bit on that score.

We dated on weekends, dances, a party or two with her friends, Saturday at the Park n' Swap. And lots of movies. Often we would meet at the local saloon after I finished my Wednesday night classes at the college. I would admit that I was much more comfortable in the pub than a few rows from the pulpit.

There is a lasting problem here, you see. I hate ceremony of any kind. It's a ridiculous little hang up for me. I will do almost anything to avoid any ceremony. I'm not really sure why, but I guess it has to do with the nuns. I hate ceremony so much I had them mail me my doctor's degree. I didn't' even like getting all dressed up in my leisure jacket. Margie once told me I looked awful in that thing and she was glad I had a blue sweater. I own one sport coat.

What was Theresa going to say when she found out that her daddy had a new lady friend? I had mentioned Margie to her, but only as a casual acquaintance, not as someone who was quickly becoming special. One Saturday I drove down to Tucson to visit with Theresa and Bill. Bill had to work, so Theresa and I went shopping. I broke the news to her and she seemed upset. "Won't I be number one anymore," she asked? She was revealing her mother's cherished sweetness. She loved her dad and she was very concerned.

"Well, what about Bill," I answered with a question. "Am I still number one or is he?" She looked at me and grinned like a skunk caught eat'n dirt. "But daddy, that's *different*, she exclaimed!

Theresa was right, of course. My new romantic interest in Margie was quite different from my love for my daughter. One in no way diminished the other, any more than my new relationship necessarily diminished my beloved memory of Marie. "You should meet Margie," I said. "She's a secretary like you. I know you two will have lots to talk about."

A few weeks later Theresa and Bill came up to Phoenix and we all went out to dinner. Bill and I couldn't get a word in edgewise. Those two chattered as though they had been high school friends. The next morning, Theresa said, "Daddy, what a *neat* lady!" I told her that I knew it from the beginning and that I was delighted that she thought so too. She still does.

I was excited to learn that there was a big Glenn Miller-type band playing at a resort hotel in Scottsdale one weekend. I took Margie there for dinner and dancing. The music was excellent. We had a marvelous time. How I enjoyed being with her!

As we drove away from the dance that evening, Margie looked across a vacant field at a lovely new Scottsdale home with a large arch over the entrance. "I have always loved arches," she remarked. "I'll get you a home with an arch," I thought to myself. But I didn't say a word. We had only known each other for about three months at that time. But, something was happening to me.

At last, something good was happening to me.

I asked Hal Naumoff, my best friend at the college (also the chairman my department) how it could be possible that I could be in love again, so soon after my time of sadness. "I'm so incredibly comfortable when I'm with her," I said. "That's what it's all about, Don" was his answer. "That's what it's all about."

I had known Margie for only about four months when I asked her if she would consider taking on a tired old teacher fellow and his two only moderately disciplined boys as permanent additions to her life. Now, I'm smart enough to know that no man ever really surprised a lady with that kind of question. Women are always about two months ahead of any man when it comes to the world of romance.

It's a female conspiracy, you see. They use all of this premarital magnetism to get a sweet, naïve, unsuspecting fellow to commit to things he must be out of his mind to consider and they are so clever that they do it in such a way that he is made to think *he* is the one who came up with the splendid idea. It's no wonder Sampson wore short hair, after he had been had.

Not that I was being dragged everywhere I went with her. I was just being led. And I loved every moment of it. Who needs a leisure jacket?

My family was shocked. Everyone must have been convinced that Donnie had overdosed on fruitcake at Christmas. Margie thought that I was rushing things. She had raised her own family. Did she want to re-enter the world of two somewhat undisciplined teenagers? That's a lot to ask of her. I was sure of that. But clearly, it was all her fault. What was a helpless, tired old teacher with two moderately undisciplined teenagers to do? I had thought of sending them to live on the moon...

A saved letter I wrote to Shirley and Joe begins thusly:

Hi Shirley, Joe and kids,

There's not much new over here in Phoenix except that:

1. I am in love (am I ever).

2. Margaret and I are ENGAGED...

3. We are buying a new home.

Shirley, "Go slow," you said. Okay. So we'll be engaged for a few months while I try to sell my place and only then will we marry, move over to Margaret's and wait for construction on our new home. How about that!!! It will take lots of doing, but it might just work. We're both VERY excited.

My God, I must have been looped! Clearly out of my gourd. Surely any fifty year-old with this kind of attitude is not in contact with reality.

Teenagers are just like that. My family must have thought, "Oh, boy, that kid is in a crisis…"

No. I had just found someone who made me happy again. I found someone who made me think happily about the future, one who eased the pain of the past. I found a brass ring whirling around me and I was smart enough and lucky enough to reach out for her (or let her catch me).

You can't plan these things. After all, we all know that love is really a form of blindness. You love what (or whom) you bump into.

When I first met Margie she was taking square dancing classes at a high school somewhere. I went with her a time or two to watch the ladies in their colorful hoop-skirts spinning around fellows in buckles and boots. Margie was always the prettiest in the hall. I took my camera along in hopes of getting that perfect picture. I must have embarrassed her in front of her friends. Her smile and laughter dazzled me. She was so loaded with charm. Her great capacity for fun and enjoyment was something to behold.

My letter to Shirley ended with the message:

> *Last evening Margaret graduated from a little square-dance class she was taking when we first met. I went to see her and she was wearing a gingham red, pink and white dress (she made it herself) with the full petticoat. She looked just delightful.*
>
> *As I saw her twirling around, ever so happy - clearly the prettiest in the hall - I felt a tremendous sense of appreciation, almost overwhelming, for her natural ability to enjoy wholesome fun. And for her relaxed friendliness.*
>
> *I told her later that I had found a gem!*
> *Needless to say, she liked that.*
>
> *Love,*
>
> *Don*

Grandpa Don met this very pretty, exceptionally friendly lady named Margaret Russell at a "Parents Without Partners" meeting in Phoenix, Arizona in 1982.

"Margie" the mother of three grown children, married Don, a widower with a grown son and daughter and twin sons who were just fifteen years of age.

Combining two families presented a challenge we've been able to survive for over thirty years. By 2013, we acquired thirty-one grandchildren and great grandchildren.

The challenge continues...

Dating "Daze"

1982

"I didn't stand a chance."

Mom and Margie's dad Arthur at our wedding in 1982

Chapter Fourteen

No Candles, No Handles

A very, very nervous fellow on his "first" date at age fifty, I found myself encouraged by a friendly welcoming hug from Margie as I entered her comfortable home on 43rd Avenue in West Phoenix. I was to learn that Margie had purchased her home in 1968 and that she finished raising her three children as a hard-working mom besieged by typical teenager problems.

She was alone at the time that we met. Deby and Cindy were both married and Keith, the youngest, had just finished high school and was living with his dad. As Margie and I got more serious about our relationship it must have seemed strange to mom's kids, having to become friendly with this mustachioed college professor with kids of his own.

It was strained for awhile. Deby and Cindy weren't sure how to read me. I, on the other hand, was trying to work my way subtly into their lives in a positive fashion, but was never sure of success. It took many years to convince the girls that I did care about them and that my intentions toward their mom were appropriate and honorable.

Even before we were married, Margie and I began to look at new homes, knowing that my Larkspur home had too many unfortunate memories to be a good place for a new marriage and that Margie's home was a bit small for us and for my boys. We would have to find a new place. If we had been smart we would have looked for a home one mile wide with rooms for the boys on one end and a wing for dad and stepmom on the other. That would have worked out well.

A townhome seemed to be the way to go. One with an arch, of course. The one we chose actually had an elegant bell-tower, a step down living room and a fireplace. It was very classy, although not real large, in a community for professional people who hated big yards and lots of acreage. Margie and I visited the lot on an almost daily basis as the home was being built.

Just after signing the initial papers for the purchase of our new home-to-be, Margie and I lingered in the model home admiring the floor plan and discussing where her favorite furniture would be placed, which rooms would be for which boys, etc. David wants the front bedroom. Greg wants a place to flop unimpeded by David. What are we going to do with Tinker Belle?

Where is Margie's treasured room divider going to go? Will it fit between the living room and the dining area? Is the kitchen table too large for the little nook at the front near the breakfast bar? Can we afford to get a dining table and chairs at this time? What color should the carpeting be? Do you think that a sheet vinyl with a soft blue and beige pattern will go with the carpet?

Sitting in the model, dreaming about our own furnishings in our own new home, I placed a small box on the table in front of Margie. "Strange things do come with this new home," I said. Then I watched as my sweetheart opened the box to reveal her new engagement ring. We had looked at rings earlier in the week and she had favored one special set, but she did not know that I had gone back to the store to buy it for her. That special moment caught her completely off-guard. What a great memory for us both!

I know that Margie would have preferred a church wedding with lots of flowers and candles. Reluctantly, she agreed to a quiet evening wedding in the yard at her home. My shyness and selfish resistance to anything that resembled ceremony prevailed. I remain unhappy with myself to this day for not being a bit more considerate. A few candles wouldn't have hurt.

However, the wedding was quite nice. Long-time friend, mother Irma played the organ for us. Margie looked radiant. The nervous groom actually looked rather dashing. The wedding guest list was small including only immediate family and closest friends and the reception guest list was much larger. Men don't understand the significance of these things to women, you know, clods that we tend to be.

I first met Margie's father on the day of the wedding. I was astounded that Arthur, in his mid-eighties, was so filled with energy as he helped to place the chairs in the yard for the wedding and reception. Around noon or so he disappeared from the scene and I learned days later that he and Margie's seventeen year-old son had spent a portion of the afternoon trying out Keith's new pilot's license in a rented Cessna, buzzing the house a time or two.

After the wedding, the boys and I moved into Margie's home and we put the Larkspur home on the market. Filled with excitement and anticipation, we waited for the new townhome to be built. When it was finished it was very beautiful. We got the keys late on a Friday evening and rushed over to the Larkspur home to get a couple of recliner chairs to put in the new house as though we were marking our new territory. It took about four months to sell the Larkspur home. Then, after we were settled in the new community, a little longer to sell Margie's home.

At last we were a family again. It was different, of course, what with our Margie working so hard at the Greyhound Tower, a high-rise at Central and Osborn, and her hubby working at the college. There wasn't much time for relaxed family adjustment. Margie had to "shape up" those boys and daddy needed it too. We all got some scrapes and bruises along the way. I'm sure there were lots of times when Margie missed the quiet of her own home.

"You're not *my* mother," the twins would complain when being disciplined. "What am I supposed to say," Margie would ask me? I, of course, tended to be a bit too lenient with them and I knew it, yet tending not to admit it. By the time that David and Greg were living out of our home, Margie and I wondered how we had managed to survive.

It's tough raising any teenagers. However, when it's in a "joined" family it's even tougher. There is an often denied but unintended natural leaning toward a little better understanding of the predicaments of one's own. That's to be expected. When dad separates his kid from the neighbor's kid after a donnybrook, he isn't inclined to automatically see the neighbor kid as the victim. Mom has that problem as well.

Through the years, as I lectured my students on parenting skills just as if I knew something about them, I suggested that disagreements between parents about how to discipline the children could be the most significant contributory factor in marriages that end in divorce. "Parents have to stick together," I often would say. "If you take the side of your child, you will join with that child in isolating your spouse," I would say. "That will build resentment."

"If mom says something is wrong and dad says it's okay, the child will be confused," I would caution. "United parents, not divided parents, that's the best way," said the wise psychologist Dr. Huard. "If you disagree, discuss it in private. Mom and dad should try to agree on a compromise decision.

"Otherwise, the child will join with whichever parent is most lenient and easy to sway, resulting in spousal isolation of the other parent. Mom, back up dad. Dad, back up mom. You each need the support of your spouse as you try to counter the formidable forces employed by your teenagers (they start at age two) to divide and conquer.

Not one prone to the degrading act of confession, I, however, would like to tell about the time I stole something from, of all places, my own church! Marie and I were at Sunday Mass with our four preteens on December 26, 1972 which was the day the Catholics celebrated the Feast of the Holy Family when I picked up a copy of a booklet filled with biblical statements that I saw in the pew. Thumbing through it I came upon the following passage from the Book of Sirach (Sir. 3/2-6, 12-14,17):

> *Blessed are those who revere their parents. A reading from the Book of Sirach:*
> *The Lord sets a father in honor over his children; a mother's authority he confirms over her sons. He who honors his father atones for sins; he stores up riches who*

reveres his mother. He who honors his father is gladdened by children, and when he prays he is heard. He who reveres his father will live a long life; he obeys the Lord who brings comfort to his mother.

My son, take care of your father when he is old; grieve him not as long as he lives. Even if his mind fails, be considerate with him; revile him not in the fullness of your strength. For kindness to a father will not be forgotten, it will serve as a sin offering. It will take lasting root. This is the word of the Lord.

Surely, you can see why I swiped this from my church. I wanted it to read in my classes. "A mother's authority he confirms over her (their) sons." Isn't this the very point of my lectures on parenting, wherein I asked each spouse to support the other?

Hopefully, God is not intent on punishing me for my theft from his sanctified home. Oh, Lord, forgive me my trespasses…

On a Tuesday evening after nearly three hours of teaching an adult class that ended on this note, I wearily closed my notes as the students filed out of the room. A petite blondish lady in her thirties remained until the others were out of the room, then she came up to the front of the room to talk to me. I saw immediately that she was very upset, tears streaming down the side of her face. "You described my divorce," she cried, "when you said that the man has to support his wife."

I was soon to learn that this lady had divorced a man she clearly loved because she could not handle the way he always sided with his thirteen year-old son whenever she tried to discipline the boy for any misbehavior. "It was the two of them against me all of the time. I was made to feel so alone and lonely. I wanted to be a good step-mom, but he wouldn't let me," she cried. "He would tell me to get off of the boy, he's just a kid, and they would laugh at me," she cried. "I still love him so, but I can't tolerate the humiliation. It's so unfair."

This is a tragedy. Margie and I agreed that it was one that we would avoid. I think I fell off the the plan more often than she did, but generally, we supported one another and stood firm in unison with respect to the rules and their enforcement as they applied to our sons. Thank you, Margie. I love you.

We often disagreed on parenting measures. But, the boys didn't know that. We didn't argue out our differences in front of them. We talked them out, compromised as best we could and presented a united front to our kids.

Even so, it wasn't easy. We made mistakes. All parents do. Sometimes we punished unfairly. Those twins could look an awful lot alike. Occasionally I would belt the wrong one. Talk about indignation! So I would really feel low.

A very special story comes to mind. Sunday morning again, wouldn't you know? Getting ready for Sunday Mass again, wouldn't you know? Chris was six and Theresa was five. The twins were less than a year old. "Chris, leave your sister alone and get yourself dressed. You know we're gonna be late," I was hollering into his room. "Theresa, stop teasing the dog and get your shoes and socks on."

"Here, honey," Marie said to me as she handed me one or the other of the twins. "Put a diaper on this one and then his over pants and top. Their baby powder is on the dresser. Don't "snuff" the dog."

I could hear Chris and Theresa teasing each other and giggling in the other room. "You kids quit that before I come in there. You know we're in a hurry," I yelled. Soon I was rushing down the hallway, carrying one twin or the other under my arm like a football, not knowing or caring which one it was. I was headed for the family Chevrolet.

Theresa arrived at the car before I got there. She climbed into the back seat and as I got there I quickly observed Chris trying to get the back door open to get in while Theresa sat inside enjoying the fact that the door was locked and Chris was locked out.

I blew my cool, tossed Greg (I think), infant seat and all, up on the roof of the car, climbed on the front seat backwards, leaned over the seat and swatted Theresa several times on the legs for not opening the door and letting her big brother in. When we drove away from the house (it's a wonder I didn't forget the roof-rider), I was probably as noncatholic as anyone could possibly be.

It was quiet in the car as we neared the church, except for the sobbing of my little girl who had been clearly offended. "Settle down, Theresa," I called back at her. "You had that coming. You could have let him in," I said. "But Daddy," she wailed in return, amidst her sobs, "There aren't any *handles* on the doors."

Oh, Oh... Well now, Dad had forgotten. I had actually gone to the Checker Auto a few weeks earlier to get caps for the inside handles on the back doors of my vintage Chevy as a security measure to prevent the kids from opening the doors in flight and falling out into the real world.

I had just harshly punished my sweet little girl for not doing something she couldn't possibly have done. What *I had done!* Oh, me. Oh, my...

How was I going to get my mean, ugly, uncatholic ass out of that one?

Talk about feeling low. I searched my head and my years of professional training as a psychologist for a cure for being a creep. I found none. Fortunately, I was able to compose myself enough to use a little common sense and say, "Honey, I'm sorry. Daddy forgot that there are no handles on the doors. I shouldn't have spanked you. Daddy is so sorry."

I was to learn a most marvelous thing about children that morning. It is that they want to be forgiving. As we slid into the pew in the crying room (me), Theresa wriggled her tiny bottom over next to me. I thought it strange that she would want to be near me after how mean I had been to her. But, there she was, snuggled close to me.

Now you know that in a Catholic Mass you sit sometimes, then at the Gospel you stand, then you sit, then at the Consecration you stand, etc. Or do you kneel for the Consecration? Yeah, that's it. Well, anyway, if you are not one of those catholics you don't understand the why of all of this up and down business. If you were raised catholic as I was, you automatically do all of this, still not having the foggiest as to why.

When we stood for the Gospel, I intentionally took a nice long stride away from Theresa before I sat down. Sure enough, with another manifestation of her mother's innate sweetness, she scooted over next to me again, the warmth of her tiny arm against her daddy.

In her childish way, Theresa was saying something very special. "I forgive you, daddy." In her childish way, she was daddy's teacher that day. I heard none of what was said in the pulpit that day. I treasure the message from the child that day. When you are wrong, admit it and apologize. And you will be forgiven. Thank you, Theresa. I love you. I love you.

Oftentimes, you wonder if the assumption of parental responsibility is really worth all of the hassle. It surely isn't for everyone. Are all of the problems that are associated with their childhood illnesses and injuries, all of the monitoring necessary to keep them from beating on one another in uncontrolled sibling rivalry, all of the parent-teacher conferences, all of the disagreements between the parents with regard to discipline just too much to handle?

Most parents, looking at their grown children, and especially enjoying the wonder of their accomplished adulthood, are most proud of their own achievement in successfully raising their kids. Most parents know that they have been facing one of the most formidable challenges life has to offer. Most meet the challenge in capable style. Most know that successful parenting results in a personal sense of fulfillment that enriches life beyond measure. As the saying goes, "I wouldn't take a million for where I've been, but wouldn't give a nickel to go there again."

Grandkids! Wow, what about grandkids? Did you know that there is no such thing as an ugly grandchild? They are truly marvelous, from Hannah and sweet Becky, Sarah and Jonathan, Jeremy and Stacia, Derek and Ann, Bobby Dean, Cortney, A.J., Lindsay, Lauren, Tyler and Brandon. They are all treasures to grandma and grandpa. Margie is the procurement director and delivery facilitator of all birthday cards. Grandpa contributes a little green. Watching the development of each unique personality also enriches our lives.

Now, we get to hear about how *their* parents are coping. Now, we get to stay at home while *their* parents untangle the sibling conflicts, attend the conferences, pay for the dental appointments and endlessly fill the empty growing stomachs. Now we learn secondhand rather than firsthand about how the children adjust to things like unappreciated academic challenges and the pain of being disappointed in youthful romantic relationships.

We hurt a little for our own kids facing parenthood during troubled times, but wonder if parents ever faced their responsibilities when times were really untroubled…

We try to reassure them that they are doing a good job. That seems to be what they need. But we willingly admit that it is comforting to us to see the tail lights of the vehicles carrying the next generation easing down the driveway and off into the distance. There stand grandma and grandpa, filled with love for our kin, but relieved to get back to TV that we can hear, our little dog that has become calm again and the quiet of our little nest on a little hilltop amidst the pines. And our many glowing memories. Thanks, Chris, for this one:

Dear Dad,

I know that I don't call as often as I should, I have no good excuse.

I can say, though, that not a single day goes by that I don't think of you. You have so much to be proud of. You have instilled in your children everything that is important, right and beautiful. This is a debt that I could never repay.

Somehow, saying thank you is not enough.

I love you, Dad
Have a great holiday season.

Sincerely,

Chris

12/25/86

Chapter Fifteen

Big Spenders

It gets mighty hot in Phoenix, Arizona. The record was 122 degrees in June of 1990. That's when anyone with any brains whatever left the city searching for a cooler climate. So it was with Don and Margie Huard who by that time enjoyed their little mountain cabin in the pines, just south of the city of Flagstaff. Not able to stay there through the entire summer, we planned every week for an early Friday afternoon escape up I-17, through the Verde Valley and into Kachina village where the temperature was usually 18 degrees cooler and the nights were delightful with smog-free skies and zillions of brilliant stars.

The building of the cabin was a fantastic idea that hit Don, Margie and her son Keith at about the time he was considering attending Northern Arizona University as a student in the highly competitive physical therapy program. We decided that if we could find a suitable lot with a reasonable price and a nice location we would buy it and put up a cabin that we could enjoy as a refuge from the desert blast furnace. Keith was eager, helping with its design and construction in return for the opportunity to live in it through the cold winter months as he attended his classes. We selected a lot only seven miles from the University.

The lot had about 20 nice-sized pine trees, a few of which had to be removed by a fellow with lots of skill with a back hoe. Next, I had to find someone who could build a level block foundation measuring exactly 14 feet wide and 28 feet in length. I arranged to meet Mr.

Gonzales, a block layer, on a Saturday on the lot to get an estimate and tips on construction.

The block layer turned out to be a Hispanic man weighing in at about 350 lbs. who worked with his little 12 year-old son. When I first saw him I began to wonder how he could manage to do that type of work and if he was killing the boy by expecting him to push wheelbarrows of cement and unload heavy blocks from a pickup truck. He assured me that they worked well as a team and the kid seemed happy enough so I hired them to do the job.

Because of my teaching responsibilities at the time, there wasn't any way I could get up to Flagstaff to check on the team progress, so I sat in the valley wringing my hands and my wallet, worrying about whether or not those two knew what they were doing as they spent several thousands of dollars of *our* money. I've always argued that as far as big spending goes, I have had to think of myself as a teacher and not as a plumber.

After two weeks went by, Mr. Gonzales called. "Hey, Donee," he yelled into the phone, "We got heem done, you see, amigo, good job." I agreed to meet him there on Saturday to give him his tear-stained check.

One quick look at his work convinced me that I had hired an unusually fine craftsman. As I carefully measured the outside dimensions of that foundation I was amazed to find that it was as close to perfect as would seem humanly possible. Every place I put a carpenter's level I saw a bubble on dead center. This man was remarkably skilled and we had a near perfect beginning for our very challenging building project.

The cabin to be placed on that foundation was designed as a modified "A" frame with ribs similar to what would be used to build a model airplane. Of course, those ribs were 16 feet wide and 14 feet high and it took considerable time to construct 11 of them out of 2 x 6 lumber, each made of two boards separated by spaced blocks two inches wide. Floor joists were also needed which were constructed by laminating three long 2 x 10 boards with two sections placed end to end to span the 16 foot width of the cabin. These were supported in the middle of the foundation by block piers also expertly placed by Mr. Gonzales and his son. We needed 11 of those joists.

Through one long winter in Phoenix, I spent every waking hour I was not teaching building the big floor joists and framed ribs in the garage of our new townhome. I built a strong roof rack for my pickup and hauled the constructed beams up to the lot each weekend, first the heavy floor joists that we had to anchor to the foundation, all spaced four feet apart. It took three or four full months to get them all in place.

Neighbors at the townhome began to complain about the noise of my saw and the hammering sounds emanating from my garage. One day I got a heated letter from an attorney hired by the president of the Townhome Management Association in which there appeared a threat of litigation unless I stopped my forbidden commercial truss building business being conducted in the subdivision. "The by-laws of the Mission Square Subdivision preclude commercial enterprise on premises," I was told.

In my counter letter, I advised them "politely" that it would have been nice if, before they began threatening me with a lawsuit, someone had asked me what I was doing. All anyone would have needed to do was walk up anytime I was working in my garage and I would have been delighted to talk about my project. I think they were a little embarrassed by their own antics.

Over the next weeks I was busy building the ribs, making up the walls and the roof. We were so excited when the first of the ribs was bolted in place so that we could stand across the creek in front of our project and see the shape it would have when all of the ribs were in place. Several months later all of them were in place and we were ready to begin installing the smooth 2 x 8 tongue and groove siding that would enclose the cabin.

By the time we began putting up the tongue and groove outside covering, the rainy season began, leaving us frantic about what was happening to our materials. A bolt of lightning nearly knocked Keith off of the roof one day as Margie and I stood in the work shed out of the rain. We were really terrified when it struck. Keith came off of that roof like a monkey jabbed by a thistle.

On the outside of the tongue and groove we put 40 sheets of polyurethane insulation, then 40 sheets of plywood, then the shingle.

Picture Margie handing sheets of plywood up to us in the wind. We would reach down and pull them up.

I chose a day when Margie had just gone into town for supplies to topple off of the roof, landing flat on my back next to a fallen tree. I couldn't move for awhile, then discovered that the only injury was a deep cut on one leg. I patched it up and was "resting" in my recliner when she got back. It was time to take it easy for a few days.

We did the plumbing and the wiring ourselves, and in spite of ourselves, we managed to do it right. What a delightful day it was when we flushed our first john and it actually worked! It was marvelous when the electricity was turned on and we could get around without flashlights and candles. What a great feeling for us when we could use electric heaters in confined areas to keep warm through the night.

"I'll design a bay window for you, Mom," Keith promised. Soon we were enjoying breakfast and coffee in the warmth of the morning sun looking out of that window which Margie framed in yellow curtains along with the doors and windows at each end of the cabin.

The cabin was actually quite small, having only one bedroom. When company came we were crowded, but happy. Keith spent three winters there as he studied at the University. Eventually he emerged from the training program as one of its top graduates. We remain proud of him for so many reasons and remember fondly the evening when we attended his graduation. He has been a practicing therapist in Tucson, Arizona for many years.

Eventually, I built a second bedroom onto the Flagstaff cabin, one that extended out over a hill on the west side. It required more piers, so Mr. Gonzales and son did more excellent block work for me. Brent, a friendly neighbor fellow, helped me with the construction of that larger room. It was a significant addition to the cabin that included a second bath and, most important to me, an excellent location for a computer and printer that I used to write my first book, a small textbook on the subject of behavioral statistics. I was very proud of that book. It became the first of a number of my worst sellers.

Laminated floor joists I built in our Phoenix garage.
Then we hauled them to the Flagstaff lot in our pickup.

Just like building a model airplane. Only bigger...

Keith - "I'll build you a bay window, mom…"

And he *did* !

Our Flagstaff cabin

Dec. 1984

We added the "West Wing" in 1986

In July of 1985 Margie and I took a trip to Washington, D.C. Married for just three years, we considered it as a second honeymoon. Our first was just a weekend drive to San Diego. Although I "enjoyed" much flying during my years in the service, I had not flown for over 25 years when we took off from Sky Harbor in Phoenix, headed for Washington International Airport in D.C. I was astounded by the power of the jet engines on the 727 and thrilled by the use of the "retro-rockets" that slowed us as we landed in a near-blinding rain after being held in a holding pattern over the city for an hour.

We were to take on an adventure that was one of the richest experiences we've had in our lives! The airline terminal was a mass of frustrated people looking for lost luggage (ours was sent by mistake to Dulles Airport) and engaging in a yelling competition for cabs as transportation to the local hotels. We joined in and after a half hour we were in a cab driven by the weirdest man I had ever seen. He had a neck nearly a foot long topped by a small head that reflected an East Indian or Pakistani heritage mixed with Oriental, Irish and Kentucky Hillbilly. His speech was totally unintelligible.

He did know where the hotel was, so he took us on the longest two mile drive that he could get away with without being caught. I tried to be friendly with him as we drove along, asking about his nice cab.

"No wrikeee Chreea Maeehooo," he responded. I couldn't understand a word that man was saying. As we rode along in the dark, the freeway lights occasionally crossed the dash of the cab and I finally deciphered the words *Chevrolet Malibu*. I tipped him two dollars which I'm sure he "no wrikeee" either.

Our hotel was ancient. The running water was rust-colored, the plumbing leaked and the beds were high humidity clammy. We stayed at that place as little as possible. To our surprise, we could see the well-lit Capitol Dome only two blocks away from out of our 11th story window. The Huards were at the very center of the United States Government!

"We need an overview first," we agreed, so the next morning we bought all-day passes for the Disneyland-type tram that tours the Washington Mall, a park-like, mile long area lined on its edges by many government buildings and monuments teeming with history and splendor.

I shot roll after roll of film as we passed the Washington and Jefferson Memorials, the Vietnam Memorial, the capitol buildings for the House and Senate, the Supreme Court Building, the Treasury Building, and the 12 buildings that make up the museums of the Smithsonian Institution. The young college girl who narrated about the sights as we traveled in the tram was absolutely brilliant! I wrote her a thank you note as we left for the day. She told interesting stories about the former presidents, past wars and kept us enthralled by the amount of her knowledge about history.

That was just day number one. Day two began with a subway ride directly to the Arlington Cemetery. Reading about it is one thing, seeing it is something very different. Thousands and thousands of white crosses covered the graves of those fallen in the service of our country, giving us a sobering sense of the extreme price of the freedoms we so casually enjoy in our everyday lives. We stood only 20 feet or so from the eternal flame that burns over the grave of President John F. Kennedy who was slain in 1963, the first year of my new teaching contract at Phoenix College.

Off to the one side, in a little cul-de-sac on a very green grassy knoll, we stood close to the white wooden cross over the grave of the president's younger brother Robert, so close that we could actually reach out and touch the smaller marble stone at its base. It brought back memories of the evening in 1965 when Marie and I and our very young family were settled into a motel in Los Angeles on a trip to Disneyland. I turned on the TV and we learned that Robert F. Kennedy had been shot by Sirhan Sirhan in the kitchen of a hotel only a few miles from where we were.

Although the Vietnam Memorial is elsewhere from Arlington, it is hard for me to envision anyone being able to forget their visit to that wall, the tribute to the 58,200 Americans lost during that ill-fated, disastrous 11-year war. Its design is quite unique. It's a flat wall of black, with a polished marble surface filled with the thousands of names ground into its surface.

Shaped like a huge inverted triangle, with its peak (the lowest part) at just below ground level, it is designed so that visitors who walk down the walkways from its narrow edges to its massive center become slowly overwhelmed by the increasing number of names they see. As one walks toward the center, he or she gets the feeling of the gradually increasing involvement of America in the war and the increasing cost in human lives that eventually ran so tragically out of control.

Each name is carved with precision. Each name must have highly significant meaning to some family in America. As Margie and I walked down the ramp we saw countless people with flowers, tearfully placing them on the ground in memory of their loved-ones. People with cameras tried to photograph individual names. Some placed paper over the carvings and tried to sketch penciled impressions of the names.

At one point, Margie stopped me to look at an elderly lady who was trying to get a picture of the name GARY LEE WHIPLE, using a cheap old folding camera that could not possibly have given her an image with any clarity. As I carried an expensive camera, I asked the lady if she would like me to take the picture and send her a copy when we returned home. She was delighted, so I had her move aside and I took a close-up that eventually made a very clear 5 x 7 enlargement that I sent to her home in Connecticut. We received a lovely letter from her several weeks later advising us that Gary Lee had been the son of one of her friends.

As we moved closer to the center of the wall, we became overwhelmed by the sheer number of names, so many sounding just like the names of students of mine as I called the daily roll for my psychology classes. There were women's names, and names of people from all races.

I felt Margie tugging at my sleeve as we neared the center. When I turned around toward her I saw the tears streaming down her pretty face and heard my wife say, "Honey, we have to leave. I can't stay here anymore." As we left we didn't speak to each other at all. As we rejoined those on the crowded tram we didn't speak for the longest time. As I write about this, I feel myself weeping inside.

Most of our nation's capital is not sad or tragic. Most of what we saw is so grand. It's proud and majestic. And expensive.

We spent the last part of the second day taking an exhaustive tour of the Pentagon. It was like a city in itself. Underneath this largest office building in the world there is a Walgreen's drugstore and lots of shops and restaurants that serve the massive military and civilian staff of 70,000 in the building every day. So many wonderful things to see!

We had two interesting experiences later in the day as we returned to our hotel. One involved getting drenched by a taxi driver who apparently disliked tourists and saw an excellent opportunity for expression. Just as we sat down on a curbside bench to wait for a bus after a heavy rain, another long-necked hacker swerved over near the curb and sent a torrent of water over us. When we came up for air, we laughed so hard that we got even wetter.

Still needing the bus ride, we boarded the late afternoon bus, plunked our coins into the thingy next to the driver and discovered that the entire bus was filled all of the way to the back with the biggest sea of black faces I had ever seen. There was not a single white person besides us on the bus, making us feel strange to be the minority in the crowd for a change. It was probably a good lesson for us, causing us to think about the isolation experienced by those who are not like most of their fellow citizens.

Day three was spent touring two of the museums of the Smithsonian Institution. We marveled at the full grown airplanes hanging by cables from the ceilings of the Air and Space Museums. Imagine a "Gooney-Bird" (DC-3) hanging overhead. The old freight airplanes from the 30s were very interesting. Also the combat airplanes from WWI, like the SPAD, and WWII, like the German Messerschmitt and American Lockheed Lightning and Mustang, were on display. I touched the Northrup Flying Wing.

The space center featured a remarkable history of all of the space flights, with mock-ups of the capsules and lunar landers. In the American History Museum, we saw the earliest locomotives, gasoline and diesel motors, the earliest generators and the experimental laboratories related to the discovery of electricity, etc., etc., ad infinitum.

Perhaps the most fascinating day for me (because of my interest in politics) was the fourth day of our stay. It began with a slow subway ride to the end of the mall that is called Capitol Hill. We visited the Supreme Court, with its marble columns and we learned a little about its former justices. It was nice to see Justice Sandra Day O'Conner's picture with the others.

Next we went to Senator DeConcini's office to get passes to the Gallery of the United States Senate. We were astounded at our good fortune when after waiting in line for about an hour we were admitted to the gallery just in time to hear our own senior senator from Arizona give a major speech on the defense budget. I was thrilled beyond words listening to Barry M. Goldwater expounding on the military expenditures. When I started to take a few notes to use in my classes I was quickly warned by a senate guard that note-taking was not permitted. I didn't argue.

After lunch in the senate cafeteria we went to the House of Representatives. They were not in session at the time. We just sat in the gallery for awhile and talked to one of the guards. We were in the very room where the joint session of congress (attended by Supreme Court justices) welcomes the president each January to give the State of the Union Address. I couldn't imagine being in the actual chamber instead of just seeing it on TV.

Later, as we strolled amidst the plush green lawns and huge trees characteristic of the mall we headed slowly toward what was to be the most beautiful building either of us had ever seen. A young lady approached us as we looked for the Library of Congress. We asked her if we were going in the right direction. That girl nearly exploded with excitement, telling us that she had just been there and that its beauty had overwhelmed her.

As we reached the steps of the building we sat resting on one of the stone benches near the entrance. The exterior is stunning to see. Then, a man in his 40s, likely a bureaucrat of sorts, assured us that we were at the right spot. As he turned to walk away, he stopped for an instant and said, "You do plan to go inside, don't you?"

Once inside the building we knew why he had asked that question and why the young girl was so impressed. The marble columns, mosaic pictures, elegant carvings and domes with stained glass were almost too much to take in in a single visit. We rode up in a tiny elevator to the mezzanine overlooking the congressional reading room. This huge room is lined by arched alcoves all around the perimeter, each with columns of ivory marble streaked with coffee-colored veins - like marble fudge ice cream. What an incredible sight! We had no idea that there was so much to see in Washington, D.C.

We saw the Kennedy Center, with its remarkable Austrian and Swedish crystal chandeliers donated in memory of the slain president. We saw the Hall of Flags and the Eisenhower Opera Theater and a fascinating replica of the carved ivory swans given to Chou En Li by the then President Richard Nixon as the first president to go to mainland China.

Back again on the subway, we went clear into the State of Virginia where we walked quite a distance to visit the famous statue of Iwo Jima. In a soft late afternoon rain we witnessed the raising of the flag on that remote island as it occurred in 1945. More history. More of what America is all about.

As our 727 left the Washington runway for our trip to Nebraska, then on to Phoenix we thought about what we had seen over a six day period vacationing in D.C. It was as if our senses had been stimulated beyond their ability to absorb any more wonder. We enjoyed the trip that much. So much the better for each of us that it was shared with that most special person.

We were in store for another surprise. The man sitting next to me turned and introduced himself as congressman Daub, a representative from Omaha, who was going home for a weekend visit with his family. As you can imagine, we talked about politics, about Watergate, deficit spending, congressional power, etc., etc.

I couldn't wait to get back into my classroom for the summer session. I had so many new experiences to relay to my students. Each one would be on the edge of the seat, impressed by my wisdom, absorbing my every word. "When I was at the Pentagon," I would say, hitching my shoulders back with an air of cultured sophistication... They weren't that impressed, of course, but had they been along with us at the tomb of the Unknown Soldier to see the precise marching at the time of the changing of the guard or had they shared the view of the Lincoln Memorial at night, they, too, would have wanted to express their feelings about the glory of America.

On a late evening bus tour taken the night before our flight home we were given a special treat by "George" our driver and tour guide. Near the Arlington Cemetery he told us to be alert as he was about to do something slightly illegal so that we could get a glimpse of a special Washington scene. "Hope the cops aren't here tonight," he said, as he slowly maneuvered the bus into the left lane and over the curb, climbing to a slightly higher vantage point. "Now look to the left, just up a bit," he instructed. "In the darkness you will see the flicker of the eternal flame at the Kennedy grave." Sure enough, there it was, a quarter of a mile away, just slightly visible as a glistening star on a darkened hillside.

I was absolutely thrilled by that sight. So much so that later I gave George a $10 tip as we left the bus. I was so thrilled that I actually lost my good everlasting conservative common sense.

Only six days in Washington, D.C. and I, too, had become a big spender.

Chapter Sixteen

A Bill of Responsibilities

For a fellow who hated school, especially high school, becoming a college professor seemed an unlikely happening. Especially when you consider that I was a total failure at anything resembling a mathematics class, not only when I was in high school but in college as well. Yet, I ended up teaching and writing in the area of behavioral statistics.

In the early 1980s my interest in the white rat laboratory and the study of operant conditioning waned a bit and I was in search of a new challenge. I had been teaching about research design and statistical analysis applied to experiments conducted by my students as they fulfilled requirements for my classes. I found that when students finished their projects they had a little more pride in their work if they could show some mathematical sophistication as they reported their research conclusions.

A t-test of the significance of the difference between sample means would be conducted on data collected as part of each experiment. I delighted in reading any student report that carefully summarized the results of experimentation then provided an appropriately completed statistical analysis followed by carefully thought out conclusions. A good report ended with "Therefore, the effect of the independent variable on the dependent variable was established at the $p = <.05$ significance level."

When I taught my first full semester statistics class, however, I learned very quickly that helping students do a statistical analysis for one study was a lot easier than teaching them a full course on a variety of statistical concepts and techniques.

Those poor students who took my first class must have really suffered. Even with my doctorate degree in research design and statistics, I was inadequate to the task. It took me at least two years to gain the confidence needed to teach that course effectively. Understanding something well enough to go through the motions and pass the exams for my own program was one thing, knowing it well enough to teach it to others was something else. The likelihood of my successfully writing a book in this area (albeit a small one) was just about nil.

My offering, *Behavioral Statistics: An Introduction to the Basic Methods of Analysis and Persuasion* now rests ignored on my bookshelf and on a few others around town. It did help many of my statistics students both during its writing and after its completion. I always felt that the book would have sold better if my publisher, KENDALL/ HUNT PUBLISHING could have put it on the market at less than the $12.95 price.

As one absent an Einstein intellect, therefore, I had to meet the demands of my profession by selling a friendly teaching style and humane consideration for the welfare of my students rather than by selling any innate brilliance. I became a plodding professor, carefully teaching step by step the mathematical skills I had to learn as I experimented with my students.

At Phoenix College the completion of my degree brought suggestions by some that I consider an application for the then vacant position of Dean of Instruction. It would have meant a considerable boost in income, but there was no way I would have taken the opportunity seriously. I lacked the confidence necessary to work in any managerial manner with the members of the faculty. I've always been a classroom teacher and I knew that administrative responsibility would take me away from what I did best, interacting with the students.

I always greatly admired those who could handle this type of work, like my friend Hal Naumoff, who served capably as my chairman, and Bob Fernie, who does so well at the same job today. But, the classroom was the right place for me.

I hated committee assignments. Every teacher has to serve on extra-curricular committees from time to time and I never found one that I liked. I served on the Editorial Board of the Community College Journal for several years. In spite of the fact that I wrote articles that were published therein (like on on marijuana legalization), I hated the assignment. Then, I served on the curriculum committee getting my statistics class incorporated into a half-dozen programs. I hated that one too.

I sponsored a fraternity. That, you will remember, was a disaster. I was too much of a loner to want to be involved with social or administrative responsibility, except for the running of my own classes where I could be the judge of what was appropriate for the development of my students.

During the 1980s, students were quite receptive to quality instruction, unlike the difficult times of the 60s and 70s when they were rebellious over the Vietnam War. In the 80s I could discuss controversial issues such as abortion, the death penalty, sexual adjustment and others without angering anyone, so long as I was very careful in my presentations.

That doesn't mean that students were always happy and kind. I had some of them quite angry sometimes, mostly because I would not give good grades for bad performance.

Several uncomfortable occasions come to mind. Once, when I was a relatively new teacher, only 28 years old, I was assigned a class in Life Sciences 191, one of the larger lecture halls on the University campus. I taught 180 students in that Introductory Psychology 101 evening class.

A young man who had a little more training in physiology and neurology than the typical freshman kept interrupting my lectures to complain that I was teaching on too basic a level. This annoying process went on through several sessions during which I explained to him that others in the class needed very systematic instruction on subjects such as neural transmission, the divisions of the nervous system, lobes of the brain, etc.

One evening, as he was becoming more annoying to me, I finally let him have it by showing him that he wasn't quite as sharp as he was trying to get everyone to believe. I didn't do it in a mean way, but nonetheless he was offended. To my surprise, one of the things I said caused the others in this monstrous class to applaud me, at his expense!

I was stunned when that class broke out into applause. Apparently they had all been turned off by this kid lectures ago. Embarrassed, the lad was quiet for the remainder of the evening. Then, at the end of class, he came up to the rostrum, looked me right in the eye and said, "I'll get even with you for that." When class resumed the next week, he was not in attendance. I never saw him again.

A rather pretty native Indian girl failed the first of my statistics exams and got very upset when I returned the tests in class. "I study very hard," she announced loudly, "I know statistics. You shouldn't fail me," she yelled as she stormed from the room. I was very uncomfortable standing in front of the room with all of the other students looking to see how I would handle the situation. I was in the process of playing down her complaint without simply ignoring it, when the door opened and I saw the student making a bee-line toward me.

I didn't know whether I was about to ingest a tomahawk or get stung by a poisoned thistle. I only knew that she had had time to get to a car to get whatever she needed to make her point. Happily, all she returned with was her textbook. She was intent on convincing me that she knew statistics. She didn't. It took me an hour after class in my office to convince her that she didn't need statistics for her program.

One day, after months of testimony in a world famous murder trial, the verdict was about to come in just as Dr. Huard was beginning a lecture before a racially mixed class of freshman students. I tapped the remote to the classroom television set assuming that everyone would want to hear the verdict. "Not Guilty!" said the jury foreman as O.J. Simpson appeared on the screen.

The one-third of my class that was black exploded to their feet as the rest groaned in disbelief. Now, I ask you, what was the right thing for the learned professor to say under those circumstances? What would *you* have said? How was I to play *that* one down? What a tortuous hour that was... There was no place to hide. How did I handle it? Miserably, I suppose.

However, I also experienced countless sweet moments through my long teaching career. Those included times when a successful student would nearly cry, expressing his or her sense of appreciation for a good grade earned by lots of sincere effort and discipline. I have a large stack of letters and cards that I accumulated over the years in which students told me of their dreams, their problems and their willingness to pay the prices for a good education. Some of the messages were quite flattering toward me. Others were not.

Routinely, we were encouraged to poll our students near the end of each semester to get comments about our teaching, the textbook and the tests used to measure the extent of their learning. The idea was to use the students' input to improve our instruction. It was helpful at times, but sometimes I found myself wishing that they hadn't been quite so honest.

On one occasion I was feeling a bit too high after reading all of the positive surveys expounding on my greatness when I turned over one of the sheets and read SUBSTANDARD TEACHING! scrawled in bold letters. That page, of course, seems to have gotten lost somewhere along the line… Let's concentrate on the "correct" perceptions, the more positive ones.

There was the memorable tiny Oriental girl who bowed before me so reverently in my office, bringing her hands together as though in respectful prayer before presenting a small carefully wrapped box to me as a gift. I opened it and found a "Thai" clip from her homeland, a carefully crafted miniature Buddha that I proudly wore to many a class through the subsequent semesters. What an incredibly sweet young lady!

"Bugga-bear" as he called himself, failed every one of my tests. Yet, he was there for every class. He was a big black man who earned his living as a prizefighter. I guessed that he wasn't very skilled, but that seemed to be the only thing he knew, so that's what he did. How or why he ended up in a psychology class, I'll never know. I'm glad that he did.

At the end of a semester, in late May, Bugga showed up at my office to tell me what a great man I was. "You a great man, man," he said several times. "You done a good job." In his hand he held a package very crudely wrapped in Christmas wrap. "This is for you, man," he said.

It was a black trivet, you know, one of those things for under a teakettle on a stove. It was square and had a square ceramic tile mounted on top, all red and bordered in white. In white across the top were the words, OVER 50 and STILL COOKING.

I would ask any teacher, how are you going to fail a fellow like *that*? I did change a few grades from time to time. That was one of them. That trivet is mounted on the wall of my office. I changed the 50 to 60 a few years later. Then, it became 70. Now, it is 83.

In 1989, I, along with a large group of other Maricopa County Community College teachers, was offered a very attractive opportunity to retire early, coupled with the option of continuing on as a half-time employee. Just 63 at the time, I felt severe anxiety over the decision, but eventually decided to join the crowd and get out while the getting was good. As it turned out, my retirement benefits started immediately and those added to my half-time salary equaled almost as much as I had been earning as a full-time employee.

Teaching only on Tuesdays and Thursdays was a breeze for the years that we remained in Phoenix. It meant long four-day weekends and lots of time for the writing projects that were becoming a more significant part of my life. I began to write mini-books for teenagers that presently sell on the Internet, with cute titles like *What Will Cigarettes, Booze, "Safe" Sex and Drugs Do for (to) you?* They added to my impressive list of fare for disinterested readers. Thus far, I have given away more copies than I have sold. I'm sure that I have cured absolutely no one.

It's been fun, however, just writing my heart out, even if my efforts fail to impress. I enjoy writing just for me. Look at it this way… Do you think that everyone who falls in love with golf and spends life chasing that little white ball around an overgrown playground gets a financial return for his efforts? Not likely. He belts that ball and walks after it, swearing over his bad shots, gloating over the good ones, because occasionally, just occasionally, he gets an enormous thrill from what he has been able to produce.

A good golfer (and most bad ones) will practice and practice, long woods, long and short irons, putters, even the ball cleaning racks just to experience a very rare shot that comes off of the turf from 150 yards out, arches beautifully on direct line to the pin, takes two bounces on the green and ends up one foot from the cup. Even if he misses the putt, he has had an experience that will pleasure him for the rest of the week.

I'm that way with words. I love words. I love language. I love verbal expression. I will willingly work for hours searching for the right combination of words that will fit a right combination of paragraphs that will make me feel just like that jubilant golfer who puts his shot right on the center of the green. I find those words occasionally. Just occasionally.

It's kind of silly, isn't it? Well, not any sillier, in my view, than getting excited by knocking down 10 pins in a bowling alley. Or, bettering one's own lap-time in a road race. And definitely it's better than blasting doves from the sky with your beloved 12-gauge.

When I was a busy young man I thought that people who read a lot did so because they didn't have anything better to do. Reading was done just to pass the time and relieve one's self from boredom. There were doers in the world like me who fixed cars and built things and then there were those who wasted their time in intellectual dreaming.

Today I wish I had spent a lot more of my young life in intellectual pursuits. Today I know that the truly thoughtful people in the scheme of things are those who have visited the worlds of others by becoming familiar with the printed word.

Today I know that some of the most productive hours of any day can be those spent with the TV turned off, with the newspaper or a book providing mental stimulation. Today I know that sometimes it's more important to think than to do. Today I know that it is much wiser to spend time thinking before we do things, reading and reflecting about the likely consequences of the things we are about to do, profiting from the experiences of others as told by the printed word.

So, I write for the teenagers about "safe" sex that isn't necessarily so and about alcohol and drugs that can destroy young people lured by the desire to be doers rather than thinkers. I resist the "Just Do It" crowd. I caution against excessive risk-taking. I encourage young people to learn from the expressed wisdom of their elders. They should listen to *me*, of course.

Once when I showed a colleague a copy of my little book *Teenagers: "Safe" Sex Isn't, But Abstinence Is...* I was told that "teenagers will do what they want to do and most are having sex anyway." The implication was that it was impossible to influence any of them in a more positive direction, therefore, why bother with such a little book.

This attitude offends me. I know for a fact that the percentage of teens who engage in premarital sex has dropped in recent years from 55% to around 48%. I feel that when young people are carefully cautioned about the dangers of casual sex, they are inclined to listen to reasoned arguments and more and more of them are making wiser and wiser decisions.

Furthermore, I find it too easy for parents and teachers to dismiss their vital responsibility to appropriately guide the next generation by assuming such an attitude. It isn't wise to give up on our kids by simply accepting their indifference to our counsel. I feel instead that our counsel is imperative, that when we become parents it becomes our responsibility to tell children that some things are clearly wrong to do, that some behaviors are unacceptable, that failure to follow reasonable rules can lead to disaster. Why, oh why, are we so afraid of saying "No" to our children?

We are overselling rights today. We are training our young to demand respect for their rights and the rights of others, yet, too many of our young people are hearing the message only as it applies to themselves. So they demand unlimited rights to self-expression that make vulgarity the common language. They often demand the unregulated right to be armed, a right that too often results in the expression of uncontrolled aggression. We see children killing children. The general population is often victimized by the exaggerated emphasis that is placed on individual freedom.

The situation is made worse by those in the media and the weapons industry who, for profit, exploit these exaggerations. Testing the envelope to the extreme has become the routine. Video games, adventure and horror films and murderous television programs are desensitizing children to the consequences of violent expression. Is it any wonder that the very nature of many young people is changed adversely by the continual bombardment of their intellects with shoot, cut and slash imagery?

Creative filmmakers hide behind an absolutist impression of First Amendment rights that should be challenged by those with more respect for the quality of the impressions fed into minds of our children. Those who insist on polluting the intellectual environment of our kids should be required to pay for their abuse, just as should those who would provide insult to their physical health, e.g., the tobacco industry.

An absolutist interpretation of the Second Amendment of the Constitution results in a fraudulent misrepresentation of the Founding Fathers' intent with regard to weapons possession in America. Arrogant gun lobbyists hate any threat to gun rights that weren't given by the Second Amendment in the first place. Anyone who carefully studies the United States Supreme Court pronouncements on this issue knows that the individual's right to own and use a weapon should be well-regulated in accordance with wisely enacted gun laws.

Any reader who doubts this should see a copy of Parade Magazine (January. 14, 1990) that provides an accounting of the Court's interpretation of the Second Amendment as stated by The Honorable Warren E. Burger, the late former Justice of the Supreme Court who served as the conservative President Richard Nixon's appointed Chief Justice from 1969 to 1986.

Still, the gun lobby promotes problem solution by virtue of self-armament. Patriotism is expressed as aggressive resistance to any laws that would regulate guns when the Second Amendment itself mandates that arms be "well-regulated."

The teaching of children to be "safe" shooters in a "family sport" is shown in nationally distributed ads as a "concern" for their welfare. It makes no more sense than teaching children to safely drive automobiles at age 10 or 12 or to safely drink alcohol, long before they are mature enough to handle the associated responsibilities.

Familiarly with premarital sex, alcohol *or* weapons by children isn't made advisable by notations about American heritage, or "family sports." They are clearly not made safe by reference to the Bill of Rights. Children should be denied access to these things until they reach some reasonable minimal age and maturity level. No patriotic service is provided to our youth by incorporating these things into their lives as "family" activities. The National Rifle Association's claim that a young person "cannot lose" while cleaning grandpa's side-by-side is stupid. Just plain stupid, yet, that's what one of their ads says.

I have often thought that those who gave us the Bill of rights did only half of what they should have done. Criticism of the Founding Fathers is akin to blasphemy in most quarters, of course, but wouldn't it have been nice if the Bill of Rights had been balanced in its effect by an additional offering, notably a Bill of Responsibilities.

Wouldn't it have been great if the framers of our Constitution had promoted the general welfare by endorsing reasonable regulation of individual rights in the interest of the common good? Today, freedom absolutists are busy guaranteeing everyone's right to do everything, when they should be emphasizing their responsibility *not* to do some things.

A Bill of Responsibilities would have instructed the American people as to the propriety of conduct that serves to promote the general welfare above the convenience or pleasures (or profit) of the individual. It would have provided reasonable ground-rules for respecting authority over license to exploit others in self-interest.

Granted, much of the achievement that is made by individuals in a democratic society is motivated by enthusiastic self-interest. Granted, most self-interest inspires production that is contributory to society in countless positive ways. But, when its creativity results in intense commercial production of violence-desensitizing junk food for the young mind and the proliferation of the armaments used for the expression of that violence, constructive creativity is not served. Youth is exploited for profit. The general welfare is not served.

Chapter Seventeen

"THAT'S A CADILLAC!"

Much of my adult life was spent caring for mom (Viola) and my younger sister Mary over a period of more than 20 years. Always close to my parents and being the oldest living in the Phoenix area as George and Viola approached their senior years, I found myself carrying more and more of the responsibility for their care.

I accepted this responsibility willingly, but found it at times very stressful, especially during those years when my wife Marie was so ill. On one occasion when times were bad, I remember visiting three separate hospitals on the same day.

Dad lived until he was 70, spending his early work career at General Motors working in the Cadillac division in Dearborn. In Arizona he opened George's Hardware in 1948 where I worked with him as a boy of only 15.

The business failed after a few years. Dad began a new career as a design draftsman at Motorola Research where he worked until he retired in 1965. He was as loyal a Motorolan as there ever was. He was especially proud of the electronic control packages that were designed at Motorola that ended up in the space probes in the early sixties. He was always glued to the television set for any coverage on space exploration narrated by Walter Cronkite on CBS.

Still, I think that he missed Dearborn a bit as well as his coworkers at the Cadillac plant. He would manifest that little bit of nostalgia whenever he saw a new Cadillac on one of the streets of Phoenix. I would watch his head turn as he drove by one of those luxury cars and he would often tell of the night that he and several others worked until the wee hours getting the first starter motor on a late 20s LaSalle in preparation for a showing the next day.

There's a very special story about my father and mother that I enjoyed telling to my students through the years. Just after dad retired at age 65, one of his older sisters passed away in Detroit. As the only son in his family he felt a responsibility to attend the funeral. He was gone for about a week and, I recall, he returned home to Phoenix on the day before Thanksgiving. He didn't know that the next day was to be a special one for him, arranged by mom (with my help) to cheer him up a bit.

As soon as dad left Phoenix, I got a very unusual phone call from mom. I could not believe what she was asking me to do. "Do you think you could find dad a Cadillac before he gets back," she asked? This from my mother who was the tightest person in the whole state... This from a mother who pinched coins all of her life, repairing already darned socks, saving the Christmas tree tinsel for years and squeezing every meal possible from anything she bought at the local grocery store. Nobody was more dollar-disciplined than mom.

Yet, there she was, on the other end of the phone, asking if I could find dad a Cadillac! I could not believe my ears. "Are you sure, mom," I asked? Those things are so expensive!" She was sure, bless her heart, and I was immediately on the hunt for the best car I could find with only about five days to find it.

I was unsuccessful the first two days as I called car dealerships and found out that all good cars were overpriced. I went to look at some and they were either abused or priced out of range. Then I got lucky. I found a retired man over near the Park Central area who had a reasonably nice Cadillac that was a bit dirty, but basically sound. I called mom and even without looking at it she told me to go ahead and make him an offer. To my surprise, the nice gent accepted it.

With only two days to go before dad returned to Phoenix, Marie and the kids and I scrubbed, waxed, vacuumed, polished, shampooed, tuned, serviced and pampered that car as it had never been scrubbed, waxed, vacuumed, polished, shampooed, tuned, serviced and pampered before.

The result was that on Thanksgiving Day we had a special gift ready for an unsuspecting dad that was as immaculate a late model Cadillac as could be found anywhere else in the entire U. S. of A! I was thrilled beyond words, waiting for mom and dad to show up for the holiday dinner and family festivities. Of course, we kept the car out of sight until after they were settled in our family room.

On a prearranged signal Kenny disappeared for a bit, then arrived with the car. He parked it in an attractive "stance" on the driveway. The car was white, with long sleek tailfins that made it look like a luxurious limo. The top was a soft copper color, with the whole package being supported by freshly blackened tires with glistening white sidewalls. I had scrubbed and scrubbed on the whitewalls, so hard that I almost broke through to the air.

"Hey, George," mom beckoned, "What is this out here? Wow! Whose car is *that*," dad suddenly asked? Dad's face looked like that of a deer suddenly startled in the night by confusing headlights. "Vi, that's a *Cadillac!*" "I know," she said, handing him the keys. "It's for you..."

I don't remember seeing mom and dad hold each other much or hug each other the way some couples do, but I did that day. Dad was absolutely overwhelmed. "I can't believe that you would do this for me," he kept repeating. Soon dad, Don and Ken, forgetting all about an overcooked turkey, were zooming up and down the Maricopa freeway with dad behind the wheel of heaven. He was thrilled to his soul by the power of that V-8, the floating ride and the thought that his Viola would have spent so much just to see him have the car he had always wanted, but could never afford.

A week later I happened to visit mom and dad on my way home from one of my busy trips to the University. As I entered the living room I encountered dad on his knees on the floor. He had the electrical schematic for the wiring of a Cadillac spread out all over the room. He had sent to Detroit for the wiring diagrams just so that he could study them.

All through her married life, burdened by too much parental responsibility, mom fought with overpowering depression. Her entire lifestyle was characterized by a sad resignation to an existence devoid of fun, joy or enthusiasm. Never was any time or money used for relaxation, vacationing or togetherness, separate from the kids. I never heard my mother sing.

The depression consumed her at times. I remember how down dad would get whenever she needed to be hospitalized. My older sister Shirley handled a lot of pressure for a young girl whenever mom had to be "away." Mom's sadness and despair were difficult for all of us to understand. It must have been especially frustrating for dad. He loved her so much, but she appeared to isolate herself from him, often avoiding any sign of affection.

Perhaps that's why that special day when mom went all out to give dad that special gift remains as such a fond memory for his children. It wasn't just a perfect day for dad, but it was a shining day for mom as well. I like to think that she was saying, "Thank you dear, for staying close to me in the troubled times."

But then, maybe that's what marriage and family-raising are all about. That *and* learning to *enjoy* life together (sadly, the part that mom and dad tended to miss out on). I wonder if mom was trying to make up for some things when I got that unexpected request from her, "Do you think maybe you could find dad a Cadillac?"

Through all of dad's adult life he maintained a reasonably positive mental outlook, considering the problems he faced. After all, he had been very seriously ill through his 40s with crippling arthritis. He did remain close to his family during troubled times. He deserved a Cadillac. Mom deserved some vacations.

I learned much about my father when, late in his life, he was the one who needed hospitalization and special care as his heart began to fail. By then I was in my 40s and was mature enough to appreciate how my parents had struggled through the years. Marie and I had our own family and we were learning how hard it is to meet the responsibilities of parenthood.

Even toward the end of his life he remained quite free of self-pity or any self-recrimination. He seemed satisfied with his life. I remember things he said to me during the final weeks of his life. "I've done just about everything that I wanted to do," he said in response to my question about whether or not he felt bitter about his health problems.

"That woman stayed with me all of those years," he said with pride when mom momentarily left his hospital room. "My boys never rebelled against me. I have had a good life." "Is there anything you want me to do," I asked? "Put new brakes on Mary's Mustang," he replied.

Mother called me early one morning and told me that dad had died during the night. To my own surprise, I felt only a calm acceptance come over me, accompanied by a gentle sadness, not any anguish, not any despair, not any regret, just the gentle sadness tempered by the feeling that his life was then complete. His was a life of satisfied fulfillment. Mary said, "Down the hall, a baby is born." That was a lovely thought from my little sister...

Mary was a divorcee with a little mentally handicapped daughter, Debbie. She and Debbie lived with mom in a mobile home in Scottsdale for some time after dad's death. Eventually, Mary met and married Roy Schmidt, a man with his own daughter and son, children Mary helped to raise.

Quite mentally challenged, Debbie required special training that was only minimally effective in helping her with her language development. It wasn't long before the great news was out that Mary and Roy were expecting a baby of their own, exciting news for Mary, who had experienced a very troubled first marriage and the sad handicap of sweet little Debbie.

On the morning that the baby was born I stopped at a florist's shop to get some flowers to take to the new mom. I was thrilled to think that Mary had another daughter. We were all so happy for Mary and Roy. When I entered the hospital room, I found Mary crying. "The doctors say the baby has a serious heart problem," she cried. "They say there's not a thing they can do."

I was stunned by the injustice of what I had just learned. I tried to console Mary, but felt incapable of doing so. When I left the hospital I pulled my truck over to an empty area of the parking lot where I had a firm and frank discussion about life with God. I'm ashamed to admit it now, but I actually screamed a curse at God for what he had done to that sweet little sister of mine who already was overburdened with impossible problems with her first daughter.

Nicole, one of the prettiest babies I have ever seen, died only four months later. Mary was courageous, as she was a few years later when Roy died from cancer. I'll never understand why Mary was given such burdens in her life. I'll never understand how a person so good could have had such bad things happen to her.

To Mary's credit, in spite of the fact that she had reason to be bitter about life, she wasn't at all. I am so proud of her. I loved her so much. Mary went to heaven, I'm sure. I'm not so sure about me, however, not the way I talked to God that day. Maybe there's a place just a little bit below heaven for people like me, for those who almost make it.

Mother's depression came back time and time again in her later life. In her 70s and her 80s she struggled with medication problems that resulted in dependency. Sometimes she would lose awareness of how much she had taken and I would have to take her to the hospital for treatment. Slowly it became evident that she could not manage on her own and that it was time for her to be placed in a nursing home.

From the time dad died in 1970 until mom's latest years, I was busy looking for rest homes. After a particularly frightening weekend when I found mom in her Scottsdale mobile home overcome by medication, Marie and I took her into our home. It soon became obvious that she could not be alone anymore and in a short time we agreed that our busy house with four active, noisy kids was not the place where she would be comfortable.

Mom pleaded to go back to the mobile home. Then I started visiting rest homes. Mom complained to Marie that Don was out "doing his dirty work." I was really hurt by that, but I knew that I had to do what was best for her so I placed her in a rest home in Scottsdale that was very expensive, but seemed to be what she needed.

Was I ever wrong on that one… Within a month we knew that the place was too big, too expensive, too noisy and too confusing for mom.

We learned the hard way that she needed a smaller, more basic care home that was, above all, quiet.

Mother wanted to go back to the mobile home. It took her a very long time to forgive me after I told her that I had sold the home and she would have to accept the fact that she would not be on her own again.

That's when I found Midge. She was a sweet lady who cared for three or four oldsters in her home in West Phoenix. Mother got the best of care there, good food and friendship. Her medications were monitored with great precision. Whenever I went to see her I found her clean and reasonably alert. She was inclined to be more accepting of the fact that she was better off there than she had been in Scottsdale.

She was with Midge for quite awhile. Those were the years when my wife's health began to seriously deteriorate. Teaching full-time, I managed to get Marie to the doctor's office twice a week and to visit mom twice a week as well. Then, as Marie's condition worsened, I found that she needed 24 hour care that I could not provide as I had to be away teaching my classes during the day.

Marie's condition necessitated the taking of medication that significantly increased her agitation and verbal activity level, a problem that quickly affected other patients in the private home where she was spending her days. Then one day, I received a call from the lady who was caring for her. She was livid! She told me that my wife had accidentally spilled a full glass of water over the keys of her precious antique ebony Steinway piano. "I want you to get that lady out of my house today," she screamed at me.

I did as she requested. A few days later I tried to get the lady to return some of the full month's rent I had just paid her, but the lady refused any refund, claiming that we had "ruined" her piano. We lost over $400. Marie felt terrible, but there was nothing we could do.

Mary was in and out of the hospital many times. I conferred with doctors for her, mom and Marie, slowly becoming a medical expert of sorts and certainly one forcibly well-trained as a social worker. In addition, there was the constant problem of money management for mom and Mary, in addition to the problem of raising our kids with Marie unsteadily trying her best to help.

When Midge decided to retire from her service as a care home person I placed mom in a variety of other homes. Some worked for awhile, others did not. In one place she was left alone too much of the time as the young couple went off to play with their church group. Then one day as I visited I noticed an assault rifle mounted on the wall over the young couple's bed and that did it. I decided that was not a good place for mom.

After Marie's death and my marriage to Margie, mom lived with Flora, a lady who owned a small home only a block away from mom and dad's old Meadowbrook home, the one they purchased just after the move to phoenix in 1947. It was on the very next street, called Patricia Jane Drive. Flora also retired after a few years so I would be on the hunt again.

Wherever she stayed, mom would get run down. She would end up in the hospital over and over again. The doctors would boost her up and sometimes I could get her back in where she was. Sometimes not. Often, it meant starting all over again at a new place.

In her mid-80s she lived with a couple who really became special. The Meyers had two private homes with about six oldsters in their care in each. They were good people. Mom was comfortable in her own little "family" with them.

Mom always loved Lawrence Welk. I bought a VCR for her and hooked it up to the little TV in her room. Then I recorded lots of Welk's programs on my set at home. Mom could never understand why his programs were always just starting as I left after a visit. Sometimes she would ask me if it was time for his program and if I would find it on her set. "Sure, mom," I'd answer. "It starts in a few minutes." That was usually at about four in the afternoon.

I pleaded with the Meyers several times to take her back after serious setbacks and they did. However, eventually they had to refuse as mom was requiring more nursing care than they could provide.

It was then that I was directed to a beautiful nursing home in extreme West Phoenix by the social worker at Thunderbird Hospital. It was the fanciest one I had ever seen and the most expensive ($3500 monthly), but they had a way that mom could be cared for there at government expense, so I set up a day for her to be transferred there from the hospital.

I went out early that day, conferred with the admittance clerk, signed the appropriate papers and waited as the clerk told the hospital that it was okay to send mom over. The clerk became very nervous while she was on the telephone. She learned, and had to tell me, that mom had died during the night.

Margie and I went to the hospital, then to the Green Acres Mortuary to arrange for her burial. Mother had always envisioned her own funeral as one held in a church with family and friends listening to the strains of the Ave Maria and Panis Angelicus sung as a tribute to her and as a reward for her dedication to her family. Surely she deserved to have what she wanted.

However, there were no close friends who still associated with this 87 year-old lady and much of her family was living out of state. Don, Mary and Ken (and Marge and Ken's wife Pat) were the only ones present at the little graveside gathering that we limited to family a few days after she was buried. We didn't encourage Ray, Shirley or Richard to come. It seemed only important that she was resting at peace with dad.

Mom didn't get her Ave Maria and Panis Angelicus. What she did get was the care she needed while she was living. She got her prescriptions filled and delivered on a regular basis. She got case after case of Ensure. She was visited twice per week and got flowers on Easter and at Christmas time. She was loved. She got letters frequently from her kids. Ray often sent flowers. She knew that we all cared.

My wife Margie helped so much during all of the years that I carried the responsibility for Mary and for mom. Margie shortened pantsuits and summer dresses and did lots of laundry for them both. Margie went on lots of hospital visits to help clean out closets and lots of shopping trips to buy panties and slips and things. Margie propped me up when the pressures got so unbearable. Margie shared our loss when mom was finally gone. My wife kept me stable. I treasure her so...

Mary eventually moved to California and was living in a retirement community where she seemed reasonably happy. She was visited often by our sister Shirley who managed her finances and saw that her needs were met. I'm grateful for my sister's willingness to assume this responsibility, more so, I suppose, because I fully understand how difficult a job it can be at times. There's always someone to confer with, always something that needs to be delivered and always the need for support from someone who is family. Rarely does anyone care for another with the same degree of concern as does another member of the family.

Mother's later life changed considerably. In some strange ways it was not as sad as in the earlier years, say, when mom was in her 70s and when she was so medication oriented. In the later years she accepted her dependent lifestyle and seemed to enjoy her family more.

When Mary and I would visit, she would occasionally delight us with some humorous comment that would never have come from her during her earlier days. She used cute phrases like "What'll I do? Mildew," when she chatted about perplexing problems.

Once, when Mary was teasing her about something and getting a little too bossy, mom exploded with "Why don't you mind your chickens and churn your own butter?" Mary exploded with laughter. Where mom got that one I don't know, but it must have come from her mother, Elmira, 75 years earlier. It was probably first said in French.

That kind of humor was buried in that woman somewhere. To this day, I often wonder why it was not used to make her life more bearable when she was young. I never heard my mother sing. I almost never heard her laugh either.

Yet, when she was old, very old, she began to accept our love, appreciate our presence, and in a subtle way, she started to play with life a bit. Her memories became more positive. "I love you, mom," I would say as I left. "You must," she would say. "You don't have to come so often," her words would say, but her voice and her tone would be saying, "Come often to see me." I'm glad that we did. Mom didn't get her Ave Maria or Panis Angelicus. She did get our presence. I really miss being with her.

I'm sure glad she gave dad that Cadillac…

George R. Huard, Sr.

Retirement from Motorola - 1965

Note 1932 Cadillac Hubcap Plaque
given by friends as a retirement gift

George and Viola Huard

1967

That's grandpa's 1964 CADILLAC !

1969

Chapter Eighteen

True Value

In 1996 I retired from my full-time teaching position at Phoenix College. A very large number of teachers quit the district that year because a special opportunity was given to anyone with over 25 years of service to retire officially and still have the opportunity to work half-time at one-half of the pre-retirement salary. This half-time salary added to my earned pension payment for each month resulted in a total income very near the regular full-time amount. It was an offer just too good to refuse.

The result was that I only had to work on Tuesdays and Thursdays, giving us many wondrous long weekends that, weather permitting, could be spent at the cabin in Flagstaff.

Imagine, a retired couple, a teacher and a secretary, with a good retirement income, a lovely home in Phoenix, a perfect summer cabin in the pines, working only two days a week and enjoying summers off! What more could we ask for?

We were surely burdened with repeated hospitalizations for my sister Mary and the constant problems with mom at that time but we were generally happy as indicated by my words in a letter I sent to my family in May of that year.

> *Would you believe that your brother is actually wearing a beard? And it looks well, generally, ah, kind of, well, UGLY to tell the truth. But, Margie doesn't think so, or at*

least that's what she says. Of course if you look like me, the more that is hidden, the better.

It was actually her idea and, lovin' her so much, I decided to go along. She keeps it neatly trimmed for me and, of course, because I have so many family problems, it is quite grey. My colleagues and students run about 50/50 on seeing me as a cowboy. A very cute little sophomore co-ed told me that I needed boots and a cowboy hat.

The ultimate insult about my beard came from, of all people, my mother! I had asked her the other day if she was going to spank me if I got out of line. "You used to threaten to spank me if I didn't bother to shave. Now I have a beard," I told her. Whereupon, she looked me over for the longest time through both of her unfocused cataracts and replied, "I thought you always had a beard." That shows how much I have been seeing her lately.

With all of the problems that we deal with these days I seem to feel a surprising sense of contentment about my life in general. Perhaps partly because of my retirement status, there is a feeling of fulfillment and career completion. Margie and I care for the same things and are mellowing (mildewing?) together. Thanks to my lady, I have the ability to enjoy the fun things, the things that are positive that help us keep things in perspective.

My son David was with us up at the cabin one weekend and Margie and I were dressed up in our western garb ready to go to the country club for a fun evening as guests of some wealthy friends. We were going to dance to the music of the Jeff Dayton Cowboy Band.

Before we left, I cranked up a good two-step number on the stereo and we gave David a demonstration of our dancing. When it was over, David went over to Margie, hugged her and gave her the best compliment she had ever received in her lifetime.

"Thanks so much, mom," he said, "for making my dad so happy."
Now, how about that?

Margie and I had had enough of townhome living by the end of 1990 and decided to get a home in a regular single-family unit neighborhood. We bought a Lennar Home on Angela Drive in West Phoenix. It was a lovely and spacious home that we thought would be the last of our purchases before we got very old. Along with the cabin in Flagstaff, the Angela home gave us everything we could ever want in the way of housing.

After only three years in the new home, Margie got a brilliant idea. "Why don't' we consider moving to Prescott?" "You must be out of your mind," said I. "There's no way we're selling this place and the cabin too." So, during the summer we lived in Flagstaff and took occasional trips to Prescott to look for land.

As I was to admit eventually, Margie's logic was correct and filled with vision. "You are getting near your full retirement and we won't be able to maintain two homes when that happens. If we stay in Phoenix without the cabin we'll roast to death in the summer. If we try to live in Flagstaff year-round, we'll freeze our tails in the winter.

Let's look for a Prescott lot, sell the cabin to pay for it, then build a home after selling the Angela house." What kind of home," I asked? "I dunno," she answered. So we started looking for land in Prescott on our long weekends. We looked at dozens and dozens of houses in the Phoenix area whenever we could get the time, trying to find a model appropriate for the pine country.

Lot prices in nice pine areas were priced out of sight. It seems that Prescott is the preferred area because of its moderate climate and clean air, neither too hot in the summer nor too cold in the winter. Eighteen degrees cooler than the Valley of the Sun in the summer, it sounded like the ideal retirement place for the Huards.

After awhile, we centered on a lovely wooded area about six miles east of Prescott called Groom Creek. It is filled with tall pines and has an altitude of about 6,200 feet. The only problem was the fact that there were very few lots available and they were very high priced.

I told a realtor that we were interested in Groom Creek one day and he asked me how much I expected to invest. "Oh, I guess about $40,000," I answered. "Try $70,000," came a booming voice from across the room. On the other side of a partition there was a realtor who specialized in Groom Creek sales. We gave up for that weekend.

We began to look for land in other less expensive areas, but none were anywhere near as appealing as those in Groom Creek.

As the summer came to its end, we decided that we would try one last weekend in the pines looking for a lot. "If we don't find something this time, let's wait and try again next summer," Margie suggested. We couldn't stay away from Groom Creek. Some fellows on a work crew building a home suggested that we find Byron Hoss. "Who's he," I asked? "He's the guy who really knows what's happening in Groom Creek."

So we went into town, located Mr. Hoss and, sure enough, he knew of a lot that was not on the market, but could be purchased if we were lucky and could afford it. He took us to the lot and we liked it. He called the owner and she wanted a staggering $58,000 for it. We gritted our teeth and offered her $52,000. She dropped a whole bunch to 57,000 and would not budge from that price. We bought it.

That was one of the wisest decisions we ever made. When the cabin sold, we paid off the lot and started our building project. Through the winter months we looked at a few dozen different model homes in Phoenix. Then, we fell in love with a 2300 sq. ft, model with a large "great room" area and four big bedrooms that had the most gorgeous fireplace we had ever seen. It would have been perfect for our lot.

Another problem. There was no way in hell that we could afford a home that large, mostly because we wanted to plan our project so that the day we moved in, it would be fully paid for. The first step was to find an architect who could redesign the home by cutting its size to about 1700 sq. ft. I found one in Scottsdale and he did it. He eliminated one bedroom, cut room sizes, eliminated the fireplace, changed the three-car garage into a two-car garage, changed the tile roof to a shingle roof, shrunk the room sizes a little more, lowered the ceilings slightly, etc., so that we ended up with the same basic floor plan covering only 1750 sq. ft.

I figured that a contractor would charge a fortune to arrange for all of the trade crews and material purchases so I decided to take advantage of some of Margie's son's advice and do that part myself. That meant getting three bids from local tradesmen for each job and making my own decisions as to which one was the best. Keith, as a builder of homes in Tucson, worked up a list of approximate costs for the foundation, pouring of the slab, framing, painting, roofing, etc., that I could use as a guide. It was most helpful.

The architect's plans had to be cleared by the Zoning Commission of Yavapai County before we could begin the project. They were apparently done so well by the architect that I had fewer problems getting approval of them than I did with the plans for the cabin in Coconino County years earlier. But then, I did those plans myself.

We had to remove trees and very large boulders from the building area. A fellow with a backhoe knocked down the trees and I found a man to cut them up and haul them away. We rented a "chipper" and we spent two days grinding up the branches, eventually wearing out the belt on the machine. Margie pitched in like a trooper on as many projects as she could.

Arriving on the lot each morning after a two-hour drive from Phoenix, we would work all day, then drive all the way back home. This went on for about four months. It would have been a great project for a couple of middle-aged people, but clearly ill-advised for me as one in his middle 60s. Within just a month or two I became aware that building a house is like engaging in heavy exercise at an advancing age. It's really good for you, so long as you don't die in the process.

By February of 1995, we had the foundation done and the slab poured. In March the framers put up the walls, roof trusses, et cetera. Margie and I spent a lot of time in Prescott "supervising" the crews. By then we had sold the Angela house and we moved into a two-bedroom apartment in Phoenix.

I kept beating the bushes for tradesmen. I needed backhoe workers, concrete workers, plumbers, electricians, a septic tank installer (I hooked up the tank myself), finish carpenters, cabinet makers, tile setters, stucco men and a painting crew. When I got bids on the painting, they came in so high that I discovered I would be paying about $200 per room for the inside of the house. "Hell," said I to me, "I can paint a room for $25, so paint I did, the inside of the whole house!

I did hire a man for the outside painting. It involved painting the stucco and all of the trim. It cost a fortune. Keith bought all of the windows from his supplier in Tucson. Some of them were very large picture windows that arrived on days when the snow prevented us from getting up the hill. There went some more sleepless nights.

At this time I was still teaching on Tuesdays and Thursdays in Phoenix. At every opportunity, we were up on that Prescott lot watching our home take shape. It was so exciting seeing the walls go up, the rooms being formed within them, the drywallers turning them into little enclaves for the big living room, kitchen, master bedroom, and even a computer room where Don would one day become a great American writer, growing much richer and more expressive in his mature years as he advised succeeding generations about the wisdom and integrity of their "Founding Father."

As the winter ended we looked forward to the warmth of the Prescott sun and the installation of toilets, a hot water tank and a heating unit to relieve us and thaw us out without requiring us to find the Jack-in-the-Box six miles or more away in town. When the hot water heater was installed, Margie wouldn't let me light it for fear that I might blow up the house and lose all we had accomplished. I could not get her to recognize that the thing was designed to be lit. "That's not a nuclear plant," I told her. "It's a hot water tank. You know, it makes for hot baths."

Rather than continue to argue with her about the inevitability of a premature July 4th, and reluctant to spend another long weekend with frigid water, I sent Margie into town for burgers and lit the damn thing while she was gone. I didn't tell her that it was cooking, but waited until that evening, turned on the kitchen faucet and called her over to enjoy the thrill of our first evening with real hot water. I quickly became her knight in shining armor.

In early June, the heating unit was installed. However, a bad igniter made it unusable for several weeks. A replacement was put on order. It was still going down into the 30s at night and we were not cleared for occupancy, so it was still off to Phoenix at the end of our working days. The framing inspector approved the construction. The plumbing inspector approved the plumbing. The electrical inspector approved the electrical system. Corrections had to be made from time to time, but we were slowly getting things completed, inspected and approved.

Most of the furnishings from our two former homes were in storage in the Prescott area. Bill and Theresa had helped us move more furniture and junk into the storage sheds than any family should ever need. Actually, it took two big sheds! Needless to say, we were getting anxious to stay overnight in our new home, heated or not.

Another idea. "It's a mountain home, isn't it," we asked? "Why don't we line the ceiling in knotty pine?" That was a neat idea, so I had the local lumber company send out a couple of stacks of pine 2 x 6 boards for the "lodge" look. What they sent was of extremely poor quality so I sent it back to them. After a week or two we got another shipment, this time reasonably good wood. My brave wife and I stood for days on hard, very cold concrete floors staining the boards ahead of time so that we would be spared the job of doing so upside down. Then we had the framing crew install our tongue and grooved ceiling.

Once up, the ceiling looked awful. The stain had taken nicely in some areas and just stayed on the surface in others. It was also much too yellowy in color. We were very discouraged at that point. Ten feet from the floor, rather than the usual eight feet, I felt uncomfortable on a tall ladder for two solid weeks as I restained that entire ceiling. It extended through both the living room and the kitchen areas. I used a home-brew of a light pecan-colored watery stain that kept me immersed in wet elbows and speckled glasses. I think my feet are still grooved from the rungs of that ladder. I know one thing for sure, my back still aches from that effort. I felt overdosed on cheap hairspray.

One very major decision we had to make was whether or not we could afford to put a really nice roof on the house. I spent many a night dreaming of how the house would look if we could top it off with a Monier tile roof instead of one of standard shingle. The price was about twice as high for the tile and I tried to remind myself regularly that I am a teacher, not a plumber. Our budget was getting strained as we neared the end of our project, we decided, nonetheless, on the more expensive roof.

When the home was done I sent a letter to my roofing company telling the bosses how delighted I was with their good work and how proud we were of our beautifully cropped and topped residence in the mountains. The management was delighted by my letter. I received a $50 gift certificate from them in return, for dinners at Murphy's, the nicest restaurant in the area. We used it to take Margie's 96 year-old daddy, Arthur, and his wife to dinner when they visited us nearly a year later.

What a delight it was when, for the first time, we stood on our new, cushiony carpet. It's a soft light copper-beige color. Imagine how delighted Margie was when I was touching up a few spots on the ceiling one day and decided to move the ladder while forgetting that I had left a container of paint thinner up top. Margie, you see, has a limited sense of humor about some things.

Once the carpet was in, Margie and I hid in the cold house at night in spite of the fact that we were not supposed to until we passed the final inspection by the people from the Zoning Commission. We cringed during the final inspection and were ecstatic when the man stapled the green form on the garage wall that indicated "JOB COMPLETED AND APPROVED!"

At last we could relax. That is after we hauled seven pickup truckloads of furniture to the house. First there's the refrigerator, then the washer and dryer. Then we hauled beds, tables, recliner chairs (for collapsing), sofas, a china cabinet, outdoor furniture, the barbeque, pots, pans, dressers, end tables, TVs, tools, books, etc., etc., ad infinitus, et absurdum, ad nauseum.

One of the best things of all, though certainly not the very best, is the fact that the day we moved in, just as planned, we were able to pay off the last of the tradesmen, laying claim to a debt-free home. The absence of a high mortgage payment made it possible for me to retire completely from my teaching job just after I turned 68. Now, with my teacher's pension and social security, we are surviving quite nicely.

What was the very best of things? Well, I don't have to look far for the answer. It's the fact that I share the home and all of the other fine things in my life with Margie, a most deserving lady who willingly took on that guy and his four kids in 1982 and slaved to keep them in shape since that time.

Margie is a charmer. She charmed us then and she continues to charm us and lots of friends today as well. She charms our grandchildren. Margie appreciates. That's important. She really appreciates what we have and how hard we have worked to get it. Not just me, but her too. She worked in the business world for many years, raising three children into adulthood as a single mom alone for 16 years before I came along. "Sixteen years of learning hard, difficult lessons," she says, and she's right. She didn't need rescuing by me.

Margie was a fully capable, highly responsible lady with a very good career, and a nice home of her own, both reflecting a life of good self-discipline, purpose, dedication, integrity and plain old spunk. She didn't need rescuing by me. It remains a mystery to me to this day why she would have taken to me, but I'm so glad that she did. I'm so glad that she appreciates *me*.

She also appreciates a telephone. I learned that fact after we moved into our home and, in spite of an order placed two months in advance, we couldn't get a phone. My Margie was like a caged lioness. Then, when we finally got one, it worked only some of the time. Whenever she felt the need to "charm" into it, that's when it wouldn't listen. It would die when she was talking to her friends. It would ring for no reason. It wouldn't work when she needed it most. I must admit, Margie was not charming at that time.

Margie has been for me, a true value. Through the hard times, when the responsibilities of my family were unusually heavy, Margie understood my commitment. Margie loved my mom, probably just because she knew how much I loved her. She was always ready to help when needed.

Life is so much better if it is shared. Not for everyone, but surely for me. I've found increased pleasure in shared achievements and lessened pain when grief is shared. Margie and I have both been through severely troubled times. We've found comfort in the knowledge that we can stand together, each supporting the other in times of sadness.

My wife was severely tested in late 1997 and early 1998 when her daughter Deby died in her early 50s. She cared for Deby until just a few hours before her death, giving her selfless love and concern (and her charm) to her family in a manner that commands respect from all of us. The loss of another daughter Cindy in 2000 was equally devastating for Margie.

I sometimes think that the true measure of a person's value is the extent to which he or she intends good things for others. No one I have ever known has better intentions than Margie. That presents a problem sometimes, for there is a saying that goes "No good deed goes unpunished." Sometimes, good intentions have brought bad results. But there is something reassuring about Margie. I know that she will never be dissuaded from trying to do good things. It's just her nature. It's part of that charm. It's a large part of why I find her so easy to love.

Margie's dad and another aged family friend, affectionately called "Poppy," who also live in Albuquerque, heard regularly from Margie over a span of a half-century. To the extent that she could, she showered them with love and affection, always making them feel important to her, which they were. They are gone now, but wherever they are, they must revere the lady with all of those good intentions.

Always devoted to her children, and also now devoted to me, Margie can be counted on. Her children knew that they had a special mom always glad to hear from them, always ready with wise counsel and never-ending interest in their lives. Each one must know that there will always be a home for them, in their mother's heart.

Margie and I have learned that we are wiser if we accept the ones we love as individuals who must be true to themselves as well as to others.

Sometimes that means that the decisions they make are not the same as those we would make for ourselves.

Accepting them and their decisions is usually appropriate when considered against the alternative, which is to criticize and challenge the integrity of them for their choices. That is a process that is likely to drive them away from us. Surely, we wish not to be the ones who contribute to increasing distance between ourselves and the people we care most about.

Now, Margie and I have our completed mountain hideaway. We have our leisure. We have each other to enjoy. We have things of true value. We have family. We know what's important, not money or fancy cars or glistening jewelry. We have family. Margie has her sewing and a cranky old man to watch over. I have a loving wife and a computer I can use to express my love for all of those who so positively affect our lives.

Why would anyone need more? How could anyone with such wealth want anything more than lots of remaining time to enjoy the wonder ?

Chapter Nineteen

Havin' a Attitude...

So much of getting along in life has to do with attitude. You can reveal an attitude toward others that works well for you or one that works against you. It's all up to you. Those who have a positive attitude are admired by others. Those who allow themselves to be dominated by self-centered negativism have a depressing effect on their families and friends. Self-pity can be a costly enterprise. Alienation is its price.

As a teacher involved in the evaluation of the efforts of thousands of young adults over the years, I had a special opportunity to see the differences in attitude shown by students in class participations and in their written work assignments. Some craved excessive amounts of attention, manifesting their need by attempting to dominate class discussions with emptiness. Others dressed in a provocative or undisciplined manner that made them appear "special," if only to themselves.

Imagine my chagrin at being confronted at the rostrum after a serious presentation by a sweet young thing painfully trying to smile and talk with her teeth artificially separated so as to impress her aged professor by revealing the tie-tack penetrating her tongue!

I have preached to electrified hair, cuff-linked ears, nearly bare bosoms, as well as neonated eyes and dirty feet. I have endured expressions of anger, confusion, indifference, neuroticism, eroticism, narcissism and pessimism as class disturbances that destroyed hours of potentially effective communication and learning.

A "special" case in point: Liz was a reasonably capable, attractive young lady who was spending a great deal of her classroom time trying to convince all present that she was worthy of special attention and consideration. Twentyish, going on fifteen or sixteen, she enjoyed toying with her professors, sheepishly challenging them to get a rise, being cute and coy, winking and squirming in provocative self-aggrandizement.

One day Liz went too far. As I finished yet another day trying to survive her immature antics in class, she came up to the front of the room to talk to me. As she leaned over my desk with the obvious purpose of revealing her uncovered, insignificant endowments, she commented about how she had "enjoyed" class that day.

She did not enjoy the rest of it. I asked her to remain after class. Following the last exiting student, I propped the door open to assure myself that I would not be accused of anything behind closed doors with a female student. Then, after a few moments of strained silence I invited Liz out onto the second story walkway of the building in plain sight of the whole world and I gave her the attention she deserved.

I explained to her that the lecture I gave that morning was not the lecture I had intended, and that she was to blame for cancelling its effectiveness. I had planned to cover the important topic of emotional attitude and the devastating effects that depression can have on personality development. I had planned to tell some personal stories about my father and his commendable coping skills. I had planned to make suggestions to my students about how to cope with overwhelming stress. "Liz," I said, with flashing anger that must have told her she was in trouble, "I had to change my entire lecture today because of your immature, attention-getting playfulness in *my* class. You think you are being coy and cute, but you are actually being a royal pain."

The girl was stunned. An hour or so later, Mrs. Halnan, another of the psychology professors at the college, stopped in at my office. "What in the world did that student do to make you so angry," she asked, having apparently heard the heated scolding that took place on the walkway. "Lizzie needed a little attitudinal correction," I replied. Liz was a model student for the remainder of the semester.

As Liz handed in her final exam on the last day of class, she paused long enough to say to me, "Thank you, Dr. Huard. I learned a lot of good things in your class."

Some students seemed to automatically search out and bemoan the worst in every life situation. Seeing themselves as victims in an oppressive society, they found excuses for avoiding any constructive effort to make things better. For them, resistant complaint, rather than constructive compliance had become the routine in their lives. Theirs was to question authority at every turn.

Fortunately, it can be reported that most did not hold that view. Most were positive, constructive and creative, some even more than their professor could have ever realized. Pierre Cozier was a student bored out of his gourd by *my* antics in class. Day after day he sat in the back of the room trying to look out the window, trying to avoid any eye contact with his prof, trying to be absent while present.

Clearly his thoughts, if any, were elsewhere. As the semester progressed I began to wonder if any teacher had ever gotten to that boy in any meaningful way. He seemed so aloof, so isolated. "How could anyone learn anything of value from such a distance," I asked myself?

I was in for a most pleasant surprise. One day, after my long walk across campus to the records office to turn in my midterm grades, I found myself attracted to the melodious sound of a distant trumpeter playing the *Flight of the Bumble Bee,* a very demanding solo, indeed. I changed my direction and mingled with the crowd applauding a very talented musician standing on the steps of the student center.

You guessed it, there was Pierre, doing *his* thing! Was it any wonder that his mind was elsewhere during my lectures? His head was filled with music. His teacher was in awe of him the day his trumpet shone so well in front of the students who cheered him on.

The next day I intentionally included the phrase "glistening like a distant trumpet in the sun" in my lecture on creativity. The face of the distant intellect turned to study me intently. Apparently, I had been wrong about Pierre. He had been listening to me all along. That was another kind of music to me.

Seeing so many differences in attitude among my students makes me wonder why some seem to have such a natural propensity to view the world sadly while others find joy in what they see, why some seem to appreciate life and reach out for their own thing while others wander so aimlessly in despair.

Psychologists have much to say about these things. Since an occasion in the 70s when I learned belatedly that one of my own students had shot himself to death in his pickup only a block from the campus, I tried to reserve some special time during each semester when I would offer support to those students who were troubled and depressed.

I emphasized the notion that some depression is a serious problem for just about everyone from time to time and that the challenge is to hang on during the difficult times until the pressures ease, being assured that, as unlikely as it seems at the time, disappointing experiences at one stage of life are almost always followed by better feelings about one's self with advancing maturity.

It takes lots of time and experience to build a stable, positive mental life. It takes courage to face the disappointments and to profit from them. Once, when I returned to my office after such a lecture, I saw an unsigned note on the clip on the door. "When you talked about young people who think of taking their lives when relationships are broken, you were talking about me. You hit me right in the center of my chest," the student wrote. "Maybe I'm not so alone, after all."

Psychologists often look upon the kind of mental outlook that a person develops as a potential self-fulfilling prophecy. They point to the undeniable fact that the world has lots of tragedy in it, lots of suffering, poverty and sadness. For so many, there is no apparent justice. For those so afflicted, there is an understandable tendency to look forward only to more of the same and a tendency to find only what they expect to find, a world to be viewed as they see it, as oppressive and negative.

However, those same psychologists also point to the equally undeniable fact that the world has much that is of a positive nature. Most people are not suffering. They are neither impoverished nor downtrodden. Most are able to see opportunity and are busy reaching out for it. Most are seeing reward for their creative efforts.

Those who dedicate themselves to the search for positive things rather than the seeming inevitability of the negative are likely to find more of the positive. It is, after all, what they are looking for.

The prophecy can be self-fulfilling. Because there are so many bad things that happen, it's easy to point to them and find proof of the idea of an unfair, oppressive, depressing existence as closest to reality. But there are also many good things in life that happen. An active search for them can reveal support for the idea that life is good, that living to the fullest is rewarded with positive reality.

The concept of attitude as a self-fulfilling prophecy has been around for decades. In the 40s it was musically referred to as accentuating the positive, eliminating the negative. In the 50s and 60s it was called the power of positive thinking. In the 70s and 80s it was called positivity thinking. Today, by Professor Don Huard, it is called *practical positivism*.

I've chosen this latter interpretation simply because I see it as a practical way to steer us in the direction of creative stability in our lives. It's a way to convince ourselves that life is worth living. It's a way to encourage us to get through life with a sense of satisfaction and fulfillment.

Look at the alternative. How practical is it to keep searching out the negative to prove how bad things are, especially for *you*? Does that approach lift you up or bring you farther down? If we tend to find the things we search for, doesn't it make sense that a search for the positive things in life is advisable?

Some of my students said that my logic didn't hold. "You can look at the rotten world through rose-colored glasses," they would argue. "You can avoid reality, making all the bad things look good."

"You can avoid reality by making everything look bad," I would answer, "when things are rarely as bad as they seem. You can inadvertently let negativism drag you down into chronic depression as a lifestyle. You can make yourself feel miserable."

Most of the bad things that we expect to happen to us never happen. Other things happen, some bad and some good, but most of the things we fear, we fear needlessly. Why do so many people thrive on their predictions of inevitable doom?

It is true that lighting a hot water heater could result in you being blown to kingdom come. But it's not likely. It is true that a chipmunk in the attic may eat a hole in the wiring, start a fire that could destroy the house and kill all of its occupants. It's not very likely. It is true that the market could crash, that the government could take away all of our guns, that an asteroid could destroy life as we know it. Positive thinkers have little time for such unlikely nonsense.

Let me alter the concept I called practical positivism. Let's think as the statistician does and stress the unlikely probability of any of those bad things actually happening. Let's call the concept Don Huard's *probability positivism.*

The probability is much higher for good things to happen than bad things. How do I know that? Well, because most people (certainly those who are fortunate enough to live in America) have good lives. Most people are prosperous and are getting along reasonably well.

If you are one who has been traumatized by life you may disagree. However, further negativism is likely to be counterproductive in easing your pain. It will serve only to prolong your depression.

I believe that a positive mental attitude is something earned, not something granted. There is a temptation to be jealous of those who are lucky enough to have it, even resentful of the fact that we might not be so blessed. Have you ever noticed that some of the happiest people are ones who have confronted life's greatest challenges? Why would *they* tend to be positive after all that has happened to *them*?

I believe it is because at some point in their lives they began to recognize that happiness is not something you get, but something you *earn*. If you work to develop it, a positive attitude can bring highly beneficial rewards for your efforts. If, by default, you don't bother to put out the effort to think positively, you can set the tone for a life of chronic despair.

If you can reach a point in life where you have so conditioned yourself toward a positive outlook that it becomes automatic to look upward rather than downward when challenges appear, to see a greater probability of success than failure, to use your attitude to elevate you rather than to bring you down, you will have won a major victory over adversity. Therein, in my view, is the key to happiness.

A person with a positive outlook sees more to gain than to lose. That person is less afraid to reach out beyond his own limitations. He (or she) is willing to take on some risk.

I often pointed out to my students my concern about the thousands of people who lived near the college who would like to do precisely what the students were doing, namely, get more education. Still, many were so afraid of potential failure that they shied away. I learned about them from students who took my radio class as a way to give college a try without having to face the competition directly. Many became quality students, joining us on campus after years of thinking negatively about their own potential.

I felt a disconcerting sadness come over me whenever a student in one of my classes began to point to today's high crime rate, the disrespect for authority, the disintegrating morals of our leaders, the economic greed of the CEOs, the government's infringement on individual rights, among a host of other ills and then suggested, "I wouldn't bring a child into this world with all of its problems the way things are today."

I think that today is perhaps the very best time in the entire history of mankind to bring a child into this world. There is less disease in the world today than there has ever been. Life expectancy is longer than it has ever been. More countries are at peace today than have ever been. There is greater international cooperation today than in preceding generations. There is less hunger today than there has ever been. More families enjoy home ownership and good jobs today than before.

It has always mystified me how so many can complain so much about the loss of their individual rights in America when they live in the country that guarantees most individual rights more than just about any other country in the world. I, as an average citizen, am free to do just about anything I choose to do, live anywhere I like, travel to anywhere I choose, say anything I want, purchase and own just about anything I like (including guns), vote any way I like, watch any entertainment I like, listen to any music I like, etc., etc. The average

American is not oppressed and restrained, but is instead more free to seek out opportunities and preferences than ever before.

What time in history was a better one in which to be born? When was the opportunity for achievement, success and personal fulfillment greater than it is today? Why are so many so busy lamenting about America's limitations when, let's face it, most people never had it so good?

It's a matter of attitude, attitude that can be positive and thus work for us or attitude that can be negative and work against us. "Well, that's easy for you to say," some students would protest. "Things are good for *you*." They may have been right. But what made them right? Was it because I had a life that was easier than most? As you've read this autobiography, perhaps you have formed an opinion about that. Perhaps my attitude is positive because I've had it so easy. Perhaps had I been tested more, I would think differently. Who knows?

I do know that those who train themselves to be probability positivists predict a higher likelihood for themselves of success than failure. They invest in what they see as a potentially expanding market. They adjust to romantic disappointments by trying again. I believe they increase the odds of success by taking the chance, by reaching for the stars. I have tried to do that.

Is it too simplistic? Perhaps. Does it hide the potential for further disappointment? Perhaps. In my view, however, it beats the alternative which is to accept a life of security without challenge.

Thomas Aquinas once observed: "If the primary objective of a sea-captain were to preserve the security of his ship, he would keep it in port forever."

Emphasis: *The Phoenix Gazette*

Parenting: A significant challenge - not without risk

By Donald Huard, Professor of Psychology
at Phoenix College

A few times during my many years of teaching, an unusual chance happening in the classroom served to make a point more effectively than I could ever have made it with even the most careful preparation. Such an instance did occur one day after I labored to make the point that the condition of our mental health is often reflected in our personal attitudes about life.

As I spoke of the responsibilities of parenthood, a favorite topic of mine, one of my young women students commented that she would never bring a child into this troubled world. "It is," she said, "just not worth the risk."

As one who "enjoys" parenthood, I found that attitude troubling, a reflection of an unnecessary negativism (called realism by some) that takes too much out of the joy of living.

At this point the dutiful psychologist in me launched into the traditional discussion of the importance of keeping a positive outlook about life, especially by anyone who assumes parental responsibilities.

Suddenly we were all started by a loud crashing sound of something striking the glass window that overlooked the campus. A large mocking bird had tried to fly into the room. All eyes were soon on the bird, dizzied by the window's abrupt interference with its flight. Again the bird crashed into the glass.

Just inside, a little moth fluttered, trying to get out of the room, trying to escape from my lecture. But for the glass, the moth would have made a suitable meal for the bird.

"Dumb, stupid bird," one of my students remarked as the poor bird hit the window again. But another almost immediately countered, "Wow! What a lucky moth!"

Interesting, isn't it, how each student watching the same scene revealed a little about the style of his own personal perceptions.

Another experience comes to mind.

During one not-so-pleasant semester I found myself hobbling to each of my classes on crutches. On my way one day, I happened upon another large brilliantly-colored moth languishing in the hot summer sun on the upper level walkway of our building. Unable to fly, the helpless creature would surely have died except for my compassionate efforts.

"Let's think positively, "I said to no one. Then, ever so carefully, I nudged it with a crutch tip toward the edge of the ramp. "Easy now," I said to myself, "mustn't damage those delicate, violet-colored wings." Gently I sent it out into second-story space where it would again have a chance for freedom and flight.

Sure enough, fly it did, glittering in the sunlight, dazzling me with our shared accomplishment. But then, another big bird suddenly appeared, grabbed my moth out of the air and munched it down as I looked on in anguished despair!

Oh, no! What had I done? Perhaps I should have sheltered the moth, not requiring it to fly. Or, would it have been better if I had just let the moth languish in the dust and heat? Was it better to give it its moment of glory, unmindful of the inevitable risk?

I'll take the glory, short-lived as it might have been. But then, I'm not that poor moth!

Can there be any potential reward without risk? Can there be any adventure without the possibility of disappointment? Can we take on the responsibilities of parenthood with complete assurance that all will go well? Not likely...

Our kids may get eaten alive by something in a hostile world. But I don't think so.

Parenthood provides the opportunity for the most worthwhile of all human endeavors. It is not for everyone. For those who choose to accept the risk, parenting gives life its most significant challenges. It offers the greatest potential for personal fulfillment.

As my children go their own ways I think positively about them and their futures. When the chips are down, they'll come through. They always have, thank you. Having held them close when they were young, fought with them and guided them through their troubled teens, I intend to marvel at the accomplishments of their mature adulthood...

For most parents the achievements of their children add much to their own glory and ease the burdens of the later years. True, the responsibilities are heavy sometimes. But, for the parent, further challenge is always there and the potential for reward is without limits. So much of it is a matter of attitude.

Surely, even in today's world, maybe especially in today's world, parenting is worth the risk.

Afterthought

Life is good, real good, almost too good. Sometimes I think that somewhere along the line I will have to pay for things being this good. I've tried to live a decent life without stomping on too many toes. I've tried to follow the rules. Maybe that's why it's so good now, because I learned the rules early and followed them reasonably well.

When I was just a youngster taught by the nuns, it was all made quite clear to me. Just be a good boy and you will go to heaven. Be bad and you will have to pay the price of eternal suffering in hell. I never did get a clear understanding of what heaven was like. The sisters gave a fairly vivid description of hell, especially when I slugged a smaller student or neglected to turn in my homework.

Heaven was seen as peaceful and fluffy, with billowy clouds. Everyone I loved would be there and those I didn't would be down below. Everyone in heaven would be happy in the presence of God. It was assumed that there would be lots of nuns there, although I often wondered why. Since I have matured, I know that that's where nuns go. God likes what they do.

Hell is harder to define. When I was young I saw it as a place that looked and felt like the inside of our family barbecue with the lid closed and me trapped above the coals with no way to get out. Presumably, no one ever came to turn it off.

I've had some time to think about those two places now and my feelings about them have changed. For one thing, I've decided that I don't really need to know what they are like until I get to one of them and then it won't matter if I don't know how the other one is.

I've grown content with not knowing lots of things. Some people have to have an answer for everything. I've decided that I'm never going to figure some things out, like how a clock can wind down without time going slower or why, as *we* wind down, time goes faster... I've always wondered how it is that marshmallows are grown. Maybe I don't need to know what heaven is. If all goes well, I'll never find out about hell.

Some people have to explain everything that is good, so they credit those things to the grace of God. God grants all good things and none of the things that are bad are blamed on him. Those evil things they blame on the devil, the one who keeps fueling the barbecue.

Maybe heaven and hell are only the conditions that we create for ourselves right here on earth. It's entirely possible that we generate our own hell when we refuse to look at how heavenly it is to be alive and well. Certainly, it's safe to say that we can make things more heavenly from day to day, for ourselves and others, by easing up on the whining and complaining. We should take the time to look at the billowy clouds above.

Now, if there is a heaven, I am not inclined to think of it as a place where you just sit amidst the fluff. Dad is driving his Cadillac all over that place! Uncle Ray will find the greatest golf course imaginable. Everyone shoots well-below par. There are no green fees. There's a huge library there with each book being more interesting than the last one.

Just inside the gate there's a Mexican food restaurant run by our friend Jimmy Ganem and his sons. It's located just on the other side of the *Toga and Sandals Shoppe*. The food is slightly better than what's here on earth even though what we are eating now is quite heavenly. The difference is that what's up there has no calories, cholesterol or guilt.

In heaven you don't have to get a haircut, or go to the dentist. There's never any bad news. You don't need to worry about offending anyone else because everyone loves everyone else. In heaven you don't have to remember to put the seat down or to put a coaster under your coffee cup. You can't make any mistakes so there's no anxiety.

Imagine - heaven hath no anxiety! That sounds great for those of us for whom anxiety was a major problem in life. I was scared stiff all through high school and definitely as a young soldier. I never took a college exam without anxiety. As a seasoned professor, I still felt anxiety at the beginning of every lecture. I'm glad there is none of that in heaven.

Looking all of the way back to my childhood, I'm kind of glad the nuns taught me to be a bit uneasy. But for anxiety and potential guilt, I probably would have said "yes" to myself more times when I shouldn't have. Maybe fear of the barbecue did keep me out of a lot of trouble.

I'm grateful for good parents and I hope that I have followed their lead. I'm grateful for my children and my grandchildren and hope that they will follow mine. Some will and some won't, of course. Some will find a better way to a good life.

I'm finding that getting old ain't for sissies. Sissies don't survive this long. Those of us who do survive don't look the way we did when we were young, like when we were 40. It could make a fellow feel downright depressed.

Not much is gained now by thinking negatively about these things. No use to look in the mirror and bemoan my aging countenance. Instead, stressing the positivism I have preached, I humbly ask myself, "Why, oh why, did it have to take me so long to get *this* good-looking?"

I don't know if I'll make it to heaven. I sure would like a chance to ride in that Cadillac again. Marie is there. I know Margie will be there too. I'm not too sure about me.

I had a delightful surprise this evening as I opened my e-mail to find that each of my brothers had sent me a nice letter. I greatly appreciate hearing from them. It seems as though each of us is "enjoying" the challenges associated with advancing age. It's a little early for Ken, however, who is only 70. He's an active dancer and is still interested in the ladies.

Biggest brother Ray is gone now. I'm 83 and my brother Richard is 88. We sure aren't kids anymore. A bit of lapsing memory is common as we age and our accumulating limitations will vary for each of us, as can be expected. Personally, I seem to be doing alright with my memory when it deals with things from way back, but am a bit lacking in more immediate memory from day to day. Psychologists (what do they know?) tell us that there is different circuitry involved in short-term as opposed to long-term memory.

It is frustrating to find it more difficult to do even the simplest of tasks, finding that what would have taken a half hour to do a few years ago now takes me several hours, with multiple breaks along the way. Getting the end of a screwdriver correctly into the slot requires careful steadying of one hand by the other. I shouldn't lift anything heavier than a package of marshmallows. A gallon of milk is too heavy. Half gallons are just about right.

The greatest challenge for me these days relates to my inability to walk as a normal person. The titanium brackets, rods and screws that were placed surgically in my spine coupled with the need to fuse a few of my lower vertebrae make my stride a poorly balanced "stumble." That necessitates the use of a walker for any short trips (except for around the house). My electric scooter helps when we go shopping, to the movies or to the mall. Margie seems content to steady me much of the time. If I permit myself any self-criticism she snaps me out of it in a hurry. "You could have been paralyzed, but you aren't." And, of course, she is right.

My surgery was not very successful. It took seven and a half hours! It was four years ago now. Pulmonary emboli (blood clots in my lungs) and a relatively mild heart attack didn't help. But, you know, these days I'm really a happy guy and am enjoying life very much.

One of the things we octogenarians have to learn is that we are not as "special" as we would like to think. A wise self-educated fellow philosopher by the name of Eric Hoffer who spent his life as a worker on the docks of San Francisco wrote that an old person must tolerate becoming common. How right he was!

It's almost midnight now and I just can't resist my urge to fix myself a nice cup of hot chocolate and to add two cookies for dunking. That's a real treat for me. Being old has its advantages. We can have another cookie... We can be forgiven for our mistakes because we are old and nothing is our fault anymore. Yet, we are considered wise, as we have lived so long. We don't have to worry anymore about dying young. I find that quite comforting. I guess that's because at 83, I still have plans...

* * *

Now, as I approach my mid-eighties, the years that are often referred to as the declining ones, I find myself feeling happy, appreciated and fulfilled. Perhaps, more than I have a right to be. Teach (convince) yourself throughout life that you are happy, and you are more likely to become so. I really believe this to be true.

To my dear, beloved wife Grandma Margie, my awesome sweetheart daughter Theresa, my fine sons and all of those who follow, know that I love each of you and wish you well. I am proud to be

sincerely,

- in the year 2015 -

your

Grandpa Don

Faculty Emeritus

AWARDED TO

Dr. Donald Huard

November 25, 2003

In recognition and appreciation
for your service to the
Maricopa County Community College District

[signature]
_____
GOVERNING BOARD PRESIDENT

[signature]
_____
CHANCELLOR

Who's Who in Medicine and Healthcare 2011-2012 • 8th Edition
From the publisher of Who's Who in America® since 1899

Marquis Who's Who, 300 Connell Drive, Suite 2000 Berkeley Heights, N.J. 07922 USA
www.marquiswhoswho.com • Tel: 800-473-7020 • Fax: 908-673-1179 • E-mail: healthcare@marquiswhoswho.com

Donald V. Huard
7305 E Goodnight Ln
Prescott Valley, AZ 86314

Current Biography:

HUARD, DONALD V., psychologist, educator; b. Dearborn, Mich., May 9, 1932; s. George Raymond and Viola Margaret Huard; m. Marie Darlene Fournier, June 13, 1957 (dec. Nov. 2, 1981); children: Christopher Leon, Theresa Anne, David Donald, Gregory George; m. Margaret Eugenia Russell, July 2, 1982. AA, Phoenix C.C., Ariz., 1955; BS, Ariz State U., Tempe, 1957; MA, Ariz.State U., 1959, PhD, 1971. Lectr. in psychology Ariz. State U., 1960–62; prof. psychology and state. Phoenix C.C., 1963–96, prof. emeritus. Emphasis editl. writer The Phoenix Gazette, 1980–81; assoc. editor The Maricopa County C.C. Jour., Phoenix, 982–83. Author: (books) Behavioral Statistics, 1992, The Violence That Prevails, 1996, Teen Agers: What Will Drugs, Safe Sex Do to You?, 1997, Where Grandpa's Been: An Autobiography, 1999, Youth Deficit Disorder, 2001, You Need a Red Hat, 2002, America's Guns & the Second Amendment, 2009; contbr. Mem., contbr. Brady Campaign to Prevent Gun Violence, Wash. Cpl. US Army, 1952–54, Alaska. Avocations: photography, travel, writing. Home: 7305 E Goodnight Ln Prescott Valley AZ 86314

Books by Grandpa Don
&
Jamie Lucier, Ph.D. (Grandpa's pen name)

May 14, 1989

Dr. Myrna J. Harrison - President
Phoenix Community College
1202 W. Thomas Rd.
Phoenix, Arizona 85013

Dear Dr. Harrison:

It is always a pleasure to commend someone who is truly a credit to his
profession. I have been attending Phoenix College since 1981. I will
graduate for the second time this May. During that time I have had the
quite good fortune to be taught by some very knowledgeable instructors.
I believe that there is always that person who shines a little bit more than
the rest, who goes that extra mile and who could be a "role model" for
many. The instructor I am speaking of is Dr. Donald Huard of your
Psychology Department.
    To say that Dr. Huard's lectures and knowledge of his field are exem-
plary would be a mild understatement. He gives every lecture as if it
were his first and his enthusiasm for his subject is felt by everyone in
his classes. Dr. Huard is conscientious, hardworking and efficient in
his work. Such commendations do not normally come so easily, but his
dedication to his work deserves respect.
    It has been my pleasure to have attended a semester of classes taught
by Dr. Huard. It will be difficult to find another instructor at any college
or University who matches his abilities. They just don't come any better.

Yours very truly,

Ann C. Justice

cc: Mr. Hal Naumoff

Grandpa Don did the contracting for
our "Dream Home" in Groom Creek,
near Prescott, Arizona.

-- 1994 --

Our Prescott Valley home
since 2006

OVER 82 AND STILL COOKING

Buffi Huard

Great Grandpa Don and Great Grandma Margie

-- Christmas 2013 --

About the Author

Donald Huard was only eighteen years-old when he was drafted into the United States Army in 1952. Frail, six feet tall but weighing only 115 lbs., Don was taunted and ridiculed by other recruits through eight weeks of infantry training followed by eight more weeks of heavy weapons combat development. He was assigned as an infantryman to be sent to Korea.

The orders for his unit were changed, however, and Don was sent to Kelly Air Force Base in San Marcos, Texas for special training as a fixed-wing aircraft mechanic. Two years of military service were spent in Central Alaska servicing airplanes used to support a Geodetic surveying team of engineers as they created maps of Alaska prior to its statehood established in 1959.

Released from the Army in 1954, Don took advantage of the G I Bill to earn an Associate in Arts degree and a Bachelor of Science degree at Arizona State University. Given the opportunity to work as a research laboratory assistant, he continued to pursue his higher education toward his ultimate goal of finishing a doctorate degree that was awarded in 1971.

At the age of 28, Donald Huard began teaching at the University as a lecturer in psychology with his newly acquired master's degree in experimental psychology including graduate level minors in business and criminology. Meanwhile, as he worked towards his doctorate degree he accepted a teaching position at Phoenix Community College where he served as a professor of psychology and behavioral statistics for 38 years. His Emeritus status was established as a retiree from the Maricopa

Community College District in 2004. His successful academic career has earned him a listing in Who's Who Among America's Teachers since 2004.

Dr. Huard's first wife died in 1981 ending a 23 year marriage. He and Marie Fournier Huard raised four children. His present marriage of 32 years is to Margaret E. Huard, who also raised three children. Donald and his wife "Margie" are the proud grandparents and great grandparents of a total of 32 children. Grandpa Don and Grandma Margie live happily in Prescott Valley, Arizona.

Printed in the United States
By Bookmasters